The PIONEER SPIRIT

A PRAIRIE PORTRAIT

Plowing

PIONEER SPIRIT

The

A PRAIRIE PORTRAIT

by LYLE ALAN WHITE

Walter Publications • The Lowell Press, Kansas City

ACKNOWLEDGMENT

This effort would have not been possible without the support and the encouragement of Koch Industries. I am grateful that they share with me the belief that we still have a rich and vibrant resource on the Great Plains of America: the people. Closely linked with the pioneers of the past, the individuals found in the pages of this book retain a way of life still rugged and a spirit still original. I am fortunate that the people of Koch share my enthusiasm for our pioneer heritage.

My sincere thanks to the people of Koch.

Copyright 1986 by Lyle Alan White

First Printing

ISBN 0-9617622-0-9   Library of Congress Catalog Number 86-82704

Walter Publications   /   The Lowell Press, Kansas City

Printed in the United States of America

To Walt:

*Whose love for people gave me the inspiration
and curiosity to go looking for Gems.*

"There's no greater thing than a friend."
Walt

GRATITUDES

My sincere appreciation goes out to those people who have given me their assistance and advice. My deepest gratitude goes out to Barbara Ann, who has participated in this endeavor every inch of the way as companion, editor, and paramount supporter. Also, Lloyd Schnell, Gary Sutton, and Gary Bodenhausen, for teaching me photography. Carl Kurtz, for showing me that there is an artist in all of us. Fred Picker and Lil Farber, for helping me refine my skills. Glenice Matthews, for her keen and timely insights. Barbara Funk and Kathy Toelle, for their sharp eyes and editorial skills. Gary Snyder and Herb Kloster, for their unwavering support of this project. There are others, and I hope they will forgive me for not mentioning their names.

And last, my heartfelt thanks to the Gems who grace these pages. They have shared with me their lives, and I am lucky for that. They deserve a lot more than thank you.

THE PIONEER SPIRIT

*H*aving grown up on the eastern edge of that great expanse of land known as the Great Plains, I have inherited and held on to a keen fascination for the prairie and its contents. Abounding with flat horizons and wide open spaces, it's a land marked by endless roads, little towns, and gritty people.

My fascination for the plains began early—in fact, with my very first ride across Kansas. I remember it vividly. I was sandwiched in a '57 Chevy wagon between my Aunt Macky and Uncle Charlie en route to my first look at the Rockies. That seemingly endless journey opened my eyes to a vastness I had never before imagined. I was out of my own backyard and out there in the wild blue yonder, rambling across the heartland.

The earth and the sky were everywhere. The road went forever. I was nothing but a small speck of flesh in the scheme of things. I was overwhelmed by space, yet it gave me no fear. There was a goodness about this big, overpowering territory. The vastness was embracing. Everything I saw looked unaffected and settled. It was a land I was later to learn "had character." And, as I grew, I developed a strong attachment to this open kind of environment. "It's a land you can't take lightly," said one native. And I can vouch for that.

Appearing forlorn and flat, the prairie is more intriguing than it seems. With an intricate connection between earth and sky, it is both colorful and unpredictable. The climate itself, with ceaseless winds, scorching droughts, and withering winters, has perpetually kept all things humble. From the outset, migrating across the Great Plains was a battle. Everyday life meant hardship; calamities were constant; staying on took endurance; claims were not had, they were won. But, out of the struggle to settle this adverse kind of landscape, there developed in those who could last an uncanny capacity to live with uncertainty. Unwavering persistence and new hope for tomorrow gave survivors a frontier kind of guts. The energy that drives the spirit became their backbone, and with their hands and hearts they put their stamp on the land. They carved out their places as pioneers.

Today's people of the plains have that same pioneer in their blood. They are the trickled-down generations from the originals, the settlers who fought the elements and stood their ground. Still aware of the balance between themselves and their surroundings, they have carried on the pioneer way by honoring the same essentials: toil, total respect for Mother Nature, and high reverence for the Almighty.

This durable way of life has set them apart, and it has been passed on. For, out of this heritage, the pioneers and the sons and daughters of pioneers have taken the prairie, a sea of grass, and converted it to their way of life where independence and productivity count. Living close to the soil, they have transformed the once Great American Desert into the breadbasket of the world. "It's hard," said a prairie farmer, "but there ain't no life like it anywhere, mister. This is God's country, and we look after it!"

Today they remain unique. Day in and day out they are the kind of people who have made this country work without the need to be seen or heard. Ordinary people, going their own way and making it count. The character they have comes right out of the rugged land they have tamed. It is pure. It is unpretentious. It is simple gumption and down-home earthiness bound into a kindred spirit. Having seen them operate, I can declare without doubt that they are a rare breed endowed with a genuine frontier vitality.

The images and dialogue that follow are an account of my sincere and enthusiastic efforts to capture some of the essence of the plains and that genuine frontier vitality: *The Pioneer Spirit.*

LYLE ALAN WHITE

Furrows, *Gove County*

SAS

Journal Entry: Mitchell County, 5/17/81

I owe Sas. It began with him. It was his farm I first got dirty on. And it was under his guidance that I learned things by the "direct method." To this day, he remains a rawboned link to pioneering. He's wiry, smart, and original to the core. His nickname itself comes from old-fashioned orneriness.

I remember the first time I got a taste of his orneriness. It was early in my prairie explorations. I was good and green at the time. One day, doing chores with Sas, he had me fetch a pig.

"Go in the pen there and get me the runt," he said. "I want to take a close look at him. Carry him upside down now!"

"Will the sow mind?" I asked him.

"Nope," he deadpanned. "She's a sweet one."

I hopped the fence, grabbed the runt, and turned him upside down as instructed. The runt squealed to high heaven, and it hit me. Sas didn't care about the runt. He was being ornery. The sow minded and he knew it. I was had. The sow cornered me and charged. I dropped the runt, straddled the feeder, and jumped the fence in a single bound. I landed outside the pen, panting from the near miss while Sas laughed til his side hurt. That was lesson number one by the "direct method."

Then there was the time he asked me if I wanted to spring tooth a patch of ground just west of the farmhouse. I jumped at the chance to plow. "Heck, yes!" I said, and we hooked up the tractor and the spring tooth and took off. At the field Sas asked me if I wanted any last minute instructions. "No," I said. "I've seen you do it. All you have to do is steer straight and follow the rows."

"You sure?" he asked with a twinkle in his eye. I should have known something was up.

I steered, spring toothed, and farmed with the best of 'em—til the last round. On the last pass, I got myself cornered and couldn't turn around. I couldn't back up, go left, or go right without damage. If I wanted to finish and head for the farmhouse, it meant taking a swipe and ten bushels of the next field's wheat. I was snookered.

When I got off the tractor to cuss and panic, I saw Sas. He was coming from behind a cottonwood smiling from ear to ear. He had watched me the whole time and was waiting for my predicament to occur.

"When you gonna learn to take instructions?" he hollered. "You can't go off half-cocked and do something as important as farming!" That was lesson number two by the "direct method."

That's how I got to know Sas so well, by the "direct method": show and tell, listen and learn, be on top of things, and go at it directly. Sas has certain instincts. He possesses the ability to be a simple ol' farmer, but yet a predictor,

Sas

a foreseer of things to come. He's always thinking. And he's right on the money with his ideas about rural life and the state of the farm.

"Agriculture is the backbone of this country," he always says, "but America is turning her back on us. Very few, besides us farmers, realize the importance of the earth and what comes out of her. Worse yet, the few who care are the wrong ones. If legislation, lobbying, and attitudes don't change, the family farm is gonna become extinct. And America will suffer when it does. You mark my words!

"We get taken for granted, by golly. We farmers may look like country bumpkins, but I say a man who can grow crops, manage his markets, and get up with the light of day is anything but a country bumpkin."

Sas says these things with a fire in his heart, and I love to listen to him when he's charged.

For me, the best times with Sas are when he's off the tractor and on the front porch relaxed, preaching about the good ol' days.

The good ol' days: before air conditioning, when folks didn't mind hard work, when a big farm was 100 acres, when you got your work done no matter what, when neighbors left their doors wide open, when hope was a high commodity, and stick-it-out was the name of the game. "Old-fashioned ways, maybe!" says Sas. "But they were worth the living. Those were the times when men meant more than machines!"

That's Sas in a nutshell—plain and simple but always on the mark. He does chores, figures taxes, welds, predicts weather, projects his yields, takes hogs to market, mends fence, and repairs machinery. He's a plain ol' farmer—maybe! But, on Sunday, after dinner when he curls up on the porch and talks about being old-fashioned, he transforms. It's when he's more than a plain ol' farmer. It's when his wisdom oozes out, and he becomes a high plains sage.

"What is the pioneer spirit to you?" I asked him once on the porch seeking prolific wisdom.

"Get out in the field and look all around," he said. "It's everything you see!"

Windmill, *Box Butte County, Nebraska*

Hunter

HUNTER

Journal Entry: Hunter, Kansas, 3/16/84

*H*unter is special to me. It has spirit of place. In Hunter, I come and go as I please, so I've got nooks and crannies that make me feel a real part of things. There're the Greiners, the Co-op, Vera's—and there are certain roads I travel and fields I walk. But my favorite place of all is just outside Hunter at the top of the hill on the dirt road that runs due north of Melvin Seehoffer's place. It's the highest point in the county, and up there you can just about see the whole world. It's where I come "to connect" with the pioneer spirit.

I was told once that when you can see the prairie, all of it, you can understand it by sinking into its scenery. I believe this because I know, more often than not, up on that hill, things are in harmony. Nowhere else does the land look as cultivated and so well kept. It's a spot where many Hunterites come to forget their hard work and heartaches and look back down on what they have. It's the niche where they can gather themselves and have some peace of mind.

Up high on that hill you can see the sky touch the earth in almost every direction. From up there existence stands out simplified and strengthened. Looking out as far as the eye can see, you can sometimes get the rare feeling that, somehow, the world was made just right. For me, and a lot of others, it's the place where we nourish our souls.

I never leave my spot on that hill without performing a simple little ceremony: I turn a slow, full 360°, looking last back down on the quiet little heartbeat I call my second home. It gives me luck. And on this particular day, in all its softness, Hunter and the land around her are as captivating as a painting—a true work of art.

Greiner Barn

Yardbirds

WANDA'S FRIED CHICKEN

Journal Entry: The Greiner Farm, as often as possible

I was rolling down a lonely stretch of two lane one moonlit night when my mind got to wandering. I started contemplating things. Things like the universe, life, death, and food. Yes, food. What if, I thought to myself, tomorrow were my last day on earth? What would I eat? What would my last meal be? I cleared my mind, my nose twitched, my mouth started watering. I laughed to myself, rolled down the window, and hollered to the world: "Wanda's fried chicken!" No doubt about it, my last meal would be Wanda's fried chicken. The slightest thought of it made me hungry.

Wanda's fried chicken is a genuine corn-fed, cast iron cooked, delicious golden brown, barnyard delight. She makes this specialty of hers from scratch, start to finish. On fried chicken day at Wanda's, you wake up to the sound of yardbirds squawking and scrambling in the coop. They're running for their lives. Wanda's out among them, chasing down the plump ones. After the right ones are caught, these hand-picked birds are undone at the neck, left to flop, then drained, dressed, soaked, singed, cut up, cooled, and fried—all on the same day. I've observed it from beginning to end: from corn feeding to pan frying, everything has Wanda's special touch. When her chicken comes out on the table, country aroma is what you smell, and golden perfection is what you get. Every single time I have it my eyes water and my taste buds throb. Wanda's fried chicken is not a meal, it's a feast. The first bite is indescribable!

Oh, Lord, on the day before I die, let me be at Wanda's feasting on her country delight!

Wanda

12

Ellis County Co-op

Willis and Janie Reimer

WILLIS REIMER

Journal Entry: The Wayside Chapel, Selkirk, Kansas, 9/24/82

*W*illis Reimer made a pact with God that, if he ever got out of the war alive, he'd build a chapel somewhere back home. "War will do that to you," he said. "I was in a bunker in Germany, and I prayed a lot. You don't go back on a pact when your life is on the line."

Willis came home to Kansas and kept his pact. When the inspiration hit him, he built that chapel he promised. With the help of Orville Schwanke, he built it right in his own front yard. "This is the spot I chose. Here's where the inspiration hit me." The Wayside Chapel is just east of the Reimer house, along the road, open to anyone who comes to worship.

One night at home, Willis got more inspiration. "Something hit me," he said. "I picked up the closest thing, an envelope, and jotted down a poem about my chapel. The feeling came right to me. I just wrote without stopping. And the inspiration caught on. Josie Glanville from Leoti, she got inspired by my poem and put it to music. You can read my poem and listen to the sweet music in our chapel by the side of the road."

The inspiration, once you're around Willis, is contagious.

Willis took me into the chapel. I read the poem, I listened to the sweet music, and I sat quietly feeling the sanctity. Willis, ever so reverently, beamed with pride. He was at peace. Not only had he kept his pact, but I could see he also was thankful for just being alive. War will do that.

That afternoon Willis took me back to the house to show me some other poems. He dabbles at being a poet. The last one he read to me was my favorite. It was the one he scribbled down in that bunker where he made his pact with God. It is a simple poem, but it's about home, and it has all of Willis' inspiration in it. With his permission:

GOOD OLE KANSAS

When the war is over
And I leave this foreign shore,

I'm heading straight for Kansas
That's what I'm waiting for.

Yes, I'm heading straight for Kansas
Where there isn't any war,

And then I think I won't
Be leaving there anymore.

PFC Willis Reimer
Hertz Mountains, Germany
World War II

THE LEANING TOWER OF KANSAS

Journal Entry: Inman, Kansas, 6/15/81

*W*inston Walker owns a monument. People call his silo the Leaning Tower of Kansas. I got directions to it at the grocery store in Inman. "The Leaning Tower is six miles north, a mile east, and a half mile south. You can't miss it."

When I got there, it had just rained, so I parked in the road and walked up the drive, dodging mud holes. At the barn, I finally looked up and burst out laughing. There it was, the oddest piece of architecture this side of Italy: the Leaning Tower of Kansas.

"You here for the look?" Winston Walker hollered as he came out of the house.

"That's why I'm here," I hollered back.

"Did it hit ya in the funny bone?"

"Have you got a hanky?" I asked with tears in my eyes.

"It's a sight, ain't it. Gets ever'body's funny bone the first time around."

I walked around it completely. It leans, from every angle it leans—it even bends. How in the world!

"What caused it?" I asked Winston. "Do you know?"

Winston smiled, scratched his head and asked me, "Do you want the scientific or natural reasons?"

"I'll take both."

"I'll give ya the scientific facts first. The ground shook, sediments shifted, the foundation went catty wampus. There was tiltin', and the holdin' bars went askew. It bent out. It bent in. And that's where she leans the most. That's the science of it."

"You're joshin' me, Winston."

"Then how about the natural causes? There's a mole underneath it, or the dad gum thing's got a mind of its own."

"I like those better. By the way, who coined the phrase the 'Leaning Tower of Kansas?'"

"I don't know who named it," laughed Winston, "but it's makin' me famous."

He rambled on. "I'm just a farmer and all this notoriety is somethin' else. It's caught me off guard. I didn't figure on havin' a first-class tourist attraction right behind my barn, but there's been more dust stirred up on my road the last six months than the last sixteen years. I figure that, if the stream of tourists keeps this heavy and farmin' comes on more hard times, I may declare this place a park, and go to chargin' for the look. They say you can really make some money off tourists."

"You can," I said, "but you're going to have to go commercial and add luxuries."

"Like what?"

"Tours!"

"Oh no! You wanna job?" he kidded.

"No, this tourist just wants your portrait with the tower. It's free, so come on out from underneath that shade tree."

"OK, where you want me?"

"Over by the barn with the Leaning Tower in the background."

"Here?"

"Yeah, that's good, stand right there."

And so, here they are, a man and his monument, preserved for posterity. Both are unusual.

Winston Walker and the Leaning Tower of Kansas

Vern of Van Tassell

Grain Elevator, *Clay Center, Kansas*

Barnstormin' Charlie Blosser

BARNSTORMIN' CHARLIE BLOSSER

Journal Entry: Concordia, Kansas, 9/18/82

Charlie Blosser is a dead ringer for the All-American airborne hero. He was born to fly.

I had a hunch I was on to another character when I got two tips about him in one day. I called Charlie from a roadside phone booth. He agreed to meet me for Sunday dinner at his motel on Highway 81 in Concordia. The Skyliner serves up some first-rate chicken and homemade rolls on Sundays. Charlie met me at the counter and told the waitress to give me special treatment. I was his guest. He insisted I have seconds, and Charlie grabbed my check off the table. Dinner was on the house.

"They told me you barnstormed," I said. "One of the originals."

"They told you right. I operated a flying circus from 1925 to 1930."

"Was it like I've seen in the newsreels?"

"Sure was! Those were the days," he boasted. "Barnstormin' was a big deal. We did the small towns, and they loved us."

"How did you get started?"

"How about I show you my sweetheart first."

We went through the kitchen, out the back of the motel to Charlie's hangar. Together we rolled out his prized possession: N4184, the Lincoln Page, built in 1928. "I bought her from the man who made her," said Charlie. "Ray Page of Lincoln, Nebraska. She's got a World War I OX-5 air-cooled engine. She still purrs like a kitten. And she's maneuverable as all get out. There ain't many like her, not left in this shape!"

Charlie put me up in the cockpit to look at the instruments and work the stick. "It must be something," I said, "flying in an open cockpit."

"Sure brings back the memories," he cooed. "You can't imagine what it was like back then. If you flew, you were a hero. It was automatic. They cheered ya when ya hit town. Barnstormin' caused all kinds of things to happen.

"Once, I was up at Ray Page's, and there was this tall gangly kid hanging around the hangar wanting to trade a motorcycle for flying lessons. You know who that kid was? Ray asked me to size him up. I met him, and I told Ray the motorcycle was a good trade. The kid was OK. He was dying to fly. I guess I judged a pretty good character then. That tall gangly kid was none other than Charlie Lindbergh."

Charlie Blosser's barnstormin' days were his best. You could see it in his eyes. When he operated the flying circus, every day was an adventure. "We flew in and out of small towns all over. We brought excitement. I got a lot of stories from those days, but the best ones have Herm in 'em.

"Herm was my barnstormin' buddy. My partner. Herm, the original, we called him. He didn't worry about tomorrow. Not Herm. He lived life on a wing and a prayer. I mean that, too. He walked the wing and jumped. I flew. He jumped. That's how we did it. Ol' Herm was a daredevil. Nothin' scared him. He was as calm as a cucumber at 8,000 feet. Back then, we'd hit a town and drop pamphlets to get a crowd gathered. Then we'd go back up, and Herm would walk the wing and parachute out. He'd parachute in a Santa Claus suit and hand out candy and kisses when he hit the ground. You should have seen it, they'd swarm him.

"Like I said, Ol' Herm was something else. He made so many jumps we quit countin'. Herm was always so calm lookin'. That always amazed me. Folks thought I was brave for flying, but I didn't hold a candle to Herm, especially since Herm had a problem. I mean to tell ya now, there was a peculiar thing about Herm and his jumpin'. He stuttered. That's a fact. Pretty bad, too. We used to tease him until he'd tell us his secret to parachutin'. He'd crack us up. You know, in them days, when you jumped, you were supposed to count to ten and pull the rip cord. Not Herm. If he'd ever counted to ten, he'd been smashed flat. Nope, that didn't work for him. We'd tease him and make him tell us his secret. This here's Herm talking: 'When I jump I count on-----e, tw-----o, thre-----e, and pull that som'bitchin' cord!'

"That Herm, he was something else," Charlie said, laughing. "Those were the days, I tell ya, those were the days. There ain't no more barnstormin', but I still fly. I take the Page up now and then. And it still gives me the same feeling. Look over there. You see my airstrip. It's unique. If you fly in here to the Skyliner, you can taxi off the runway right up to your motel room. It's the only one I know of. First-class convenience for pilots. That's my way of helping flyers be close to the ground and the wild blue yonder at the same time."

"And what about the Lincoln Page?" I asked him. "When are you taking her up again?" "Real soon," said Charlie. "In fact, I oughta get her back out and rev her up. Charlie Blosser Day is coming up. Here in Concordia, they still look at me as some sorta hero."

"No kidding," I said. "Barnstormin's made you famous. I wonder what Herm would think."

"If Ol' Herm were here," said Charlie, "I guarantee ya, no matter what shape he'd be in, he'd wanna walk the wing and jump!"

Storm, *Ness County*

Gus

GUS

Journal Entry: Hunter, 8/10/82

*G*us Dieter and I go way back. He might be the first person I ever met in Hunter. Gus and I have played snooker together, treed coons, driven the back roads, and the two of us have occasionally been responsible for getting things riled up at Vera's on Saturday nights.

The only cockfight I ever saw was with Gus. It was in a barn with hay bales for stands and a pit of straw. All of us there had "fightin' roosters" out of the batch Gus himself had raised. He was proud of them. He gave me the pick of the bunch. I called my rooster KC after my hometown. We bet dollar bills and swigs of elderberry wine on whose rooster would win by knockdown or by stirring up the most dust. We didn't fight them to the death. I couldn't handle that. And Gus likes to take his roosters home.

Gus and I had our own little bet. The winner of our fight got the money, the roosters, and the rest of the wine. Gus won fair and square. I was glad he got my rooster and the rest of the wine, but I still pester him about KC, the cock that wouldn't come out and fight.

I came to Gus' rescue once, too. He was coming to see Doug and me during the rowdy days of college. Gus never traveled much, so it was quite a deal at the time. In those days, you drank beer and showed off on Friday nights, and Gus was going to join us for once. He never made it, though. He got to the edge of Hays and was stopped for weaving and driving left of the center line.

After the sobriety test, the friendly officer took him straight to jail. Captain Younger called us and spoiled everything. He told Doug and me, "Your buddy is a hazard." According to his Ellis County breathalizer test, Gus ought to be dead. We couldn't figure it. We told Captain Younger that Gus could hold a lot, and he could always drive. Gus even admitted it was only a case of beer. "It was probably the altitude," we told Captain Younger, but he didn't buy it. He told us to get Gus to bed or out of town because he didn't want him passing out and not waking up. "I won't have him dying in *my* jail!" he declared.

You should have seen Gus. The altitude had him all right. He was wiped out. This story is one of our classics. And to this day, there are ramifications on Gus and his travels. It takes a wedding or a funeral to get him out of the county now. If you want Gus Dieter these days, you've got to go and see him.

Gus works every day at the Co-op station in Hunter. He's probably repaired every tire in Mitchell County at least once. I always stop in the station first thing to see him and to get a good story, too. You see, in Hunter, if you want a good story, you go to the Co-op station. The boys there keep a bead on things. Let me make it clear and in accordance with the boys: at the Co-op you don't hear gossip—women do that. At the Co-op you hear real live stories!

So this day, I stop in the Co-op bright and early. Gus is over by the tire rack stacking some tubes. I say hello to everybody and go over to where Gus is, and I see straight away my ol' buddy has one hellacious shiner. I say to him, "Geez, Gus, what did you get in the way of?"

"Just a tire iron," he mumbles. "It flew up and smacked me. . . ." I look out of the corner of my eye where a few of the boys are sitting, and I see snickering galore. I know something is up. A good story. So I mosey over to the boys to get the lowdown.

Guess what! Contrary to Gus' story of the flying tire iron, the boys have a different version. They claim Gus got his shiner at home from a flying rolling pin and a raging wife. That's what they claim! The only proven fact is that the shiner appeared around quitting time when no one but Gus was around, so either version is possible. For certain, we've got a controversy here. The accusations and raillery will be hot and heavy until the truth comes out or the shiner goes down.

That's how it is in a small town like Hunter. It's an event, something unusual like this. People out here live on gossip, and everyone eventually has his day. In small-town America, you've got to expect some razzing when things aren't normal. It adds spice to life. You take Gus and his shiner. It's a big deal. Reputations are at stake. Gus stands firm. He's not about to admit to anything but the tire tool tale. His pride is on the line. Everybody else in town just lift their eyebrows and chuckle. "Go on, Gus," the boys teased him this morning. "Tell L.A. how you really got the shiner!" Gus either paid no attention to them or said two words: "tire iron."

On this one, I have to take sides. I look hard at the faces of the boys and, then, at Gus. I stare at his shiner and the sheepish smile on his face. I can't help but laugh. If I have to bet the farm on this one, I won't put my money on my ol' buddy Gus. No way. He's got home written all over that shiner, and the boys and I know it!

Pig Portrait, *Mitchell County*

Elmer Stump

ELMER STUMP

Journal Entry: Highway 181, 10/17/81

*E*lmer Stump was putting up fence along 181 north of Lebanon when I spotted him. I pulled off the highway and went to him looking for directions. I could tell he was a quiet man. I would have to prod him to speak.

"Where's the cafe?" I asked.

"Back south to town, then left at the main corner. Can't miss it."

"Is this your land?"

"Yes, sir."

"Do you mind if I ask you a few things about it? I'm interested in people who've had their roots on the Great Plains. Were you brought up here?"

"Sure was! This land's been in my family for generations."

"Then you're a pioneer."

"I reckon I am."

"What does your land mean to you?"

"Well, you know, I've never given it deep thought," said Elmer. "On account I'd never sell it or change the way it's been in my family. Our land is something that's handed down. Once you got it, you work it, then you pass it on. I'd say there's still pioneer in it, since it's handed down. This ground's got roots—Stump roots!"

"So you never considered selling out in the harder times?"

"No, land means more than that. It has a value worth more than money. But I did leave for a time, left the land I was raised on. I was your prodigal son once. I went out and seen the world. I worked at Sears. I taught school. And I traveled. I've seen the whole country, but that didn't change me from coming home. I always knew I'd come back. And now I'm here, home for good, home to roost!"

"So, if I offered you top dollar for your land, right now, you still wouldn't sell?"

"No, no way. Money ain't everything. I got some of my dad in me. Now, he was a pioneer! My dad, he knew every letter of the word *work*—frontwards and backwards. I remember those times when we didn't have a thing. We had to eke out a livin' from nothin'. My dad, he never gave up, never packed it in. I remember when I was a kid, right here in this field, dad picked up a clod and said, 'It ain't much, but it's mine!' You don't forget things like that. And you don't sell out your heritage just to be a man who can buy what he wants to. Outta respect, this land will never be sold, not by Elmer Stump!"

ARTHUR SAYLER

Journal Entry: Albert, Kansas, 5/31/83

*A*rthur Sayler is a dandy. I never met a man more content. His mere presence has curative effects. I followed him around today, and before it was over I found myself whistling and humming tunes like he was. He hummed in the yard. He whistled in the barn. He did both on the porch where we had lunch. "Arthur wasn't putting on just for you," his wife told me. "He whistles and hums every day. Nothin' raggles him. He's perpetually happy. He's been like this for years."

Softhearted and easygoing, I found that Arthur has something special. This one rare quality. He makes time for life. He enjoys every moment of the day. "Life's been good to me," he said. Just to watch him scoot around the barnyard so content is a shot in the arm for ordinary life. Arthur and his humming can make you forget about taxes, bombs, and bills, if only for a day. They ought to take some of his good nature, bottle it, and put it on the market. The world would be better for it.

"Friendliness is a virtue," says Arthur. "And the good life is my good fortune, and it can be anybody's. It's really pretty simple: be kind, be ready to help, and don't go fast. That's how I made it. That's where my fortune lies."

POSTSCRIPT:

Good Ol' Arthur sent me a card for Christmas. He wrote: "Lyle, I'll never forget the wonderful day we spent together. You were good company. I learned from you." Imagine that! I sent him a Christmas card saying the same thing, plus "Arthur, thanks to you, I'm still humming."

Arthur Sayler

January Train

THE A TRAIN

Journal Entry: Cassoday, Kansas, 10/11/82

*T*his once, I hung around the old train station all day waiting for the freighter to roll by. I was here for sentimental reasons. I wanted to feel the ground tremble. I wanted to be blown back by the force of the wind. I wanted to get as close as I could, just for the memories of a train.

When I was a kid, I used to live at the tracks. That's where the freighter rolled by. My buddies and I had a regular ritual with the train. When we heard the afternoon express with its whistle blasting in the distance, we would drop everything else and head for our spot. Our challenge was to get there just in the nick of time and see which one of us could stand on the rail the longest without falling off or being scared. We would bet against each other with pennies. We would balance ourselves until the oncoming vibrations made our teeth chatter.

But then, when the whistle got loud and the express loomed large on the horizon, we all scattered like rabbits. The mighty train would roar by as a blur, and from back behind the bushes we would stare. It was an awesome power. The ties jiggled, the ground quaked, and the bushes blew. It affected everything not bolted down. It was a thrill to feel the force of the freighter. Every single time it gave us goose bumps.

In the bushes we argued about our bets: who balanced best on the rail or who was "not chicken" longest. No one ever won. We were all just as scared. We all kept our pennies except for the one we laid down on the track.

The thrill ended with us picking up the penny. It would be smashed flat. Then we would wave at the brakeman in the faded red caboose. He always waved back. This was our regular ritual back then. Today the A train brought it all back.

The A Train

Cimarron Sunrise

JOHN HARBISON

Journal Entry: Florence, Kansas, 7/21/81

I spotted John Harbison from the dusty road that passes his place. He was watering his garden in the misery of July heat. The day was a broiler. There wasn't a cloud in the sky. It was dry as a bone, and the temperature was blistering. I saw John, and it struck me as unusual—a human being outdoors on a day like this. His presence defied misery. This gave me the urge to stop. To get acquainted, I pulled up into his drive, got out, and told him I was lost. He looked at me like I was crazed by the heat.

"It's hard to get lost around here," he said. "Where you headed?"

"Florence."

"You're on the right road, sure enough. Stay south," he said. "It's hot enough to fry an egg on the asphalt, ain't it? How about some water? Would you like a drink?"

"I'd like a drink. In fact, I'd love some really cold water."

"By the way, my name's Harbison, John Harbison. I've been around these parts seventy-five years. Do you get lost much?"

"Only when I'm hot and thirsty!"

John laughed and handed me a big jug of water from his well. "Here ya go. How's that?"

"Divine."

"Around Florence we're known for our water. Some say it's the sweetest anywhere. It's been tested 99 percent pure. Take a big swig of it. Ain't it sweet?

"I was at a picnic once, braggin' about our water, and this ol' boy called my bluff. He said, 'Water's water, ain't no difference.' Well, we'll just see, I told him. We went and got some city water and some of my well water and had folks try 'em both. They all said my water was better, a lot better. That's proof! Here, let me get you another jug of it."

My hunch was right. The urge to stop had substance. I had gotten lost in a good place. John Harbison has this crackling sort of energy. He rose above the heat. Taking off his straw hat and dabbing his brow with a bandana, he said to me: "You can't let the elements get ya, not out here in the wide open spaces. This is the country. We're smack in the middle of the plains and the weather can test ya. If you let heat, cold, and wind bother ya out here, you can be mad all the time. Nope, you gotta ignore the extremes!"

John's wife brought us a fresh jug of water and got after us to get in the shade. We went over and sat in some country air conditioning, a rock garden under an elm. It had shade. Boy, you could feel the difference.

"John," I said, "I don't know if it's the dust, the heat, or the story you told, but this is the best liquid I've ever put down my dry parched throat. It makes me glad I got lost . . . on purpose."

John Harbison

John laughed. "On purpose! I didn't think you looked lost when you pulled in here. You rascal, you know your way around, don't ya?"

"There's an art to getting lost," I said.

In the shade we relaxed and loosened up. John chewed on a piece of grass. I gulped water and admired his garden.

"You've got quite a collection of rocks here, John. Is that big one over there petrified wood? It looks like it."

"Yes, sir, petrified wood it is. A real museum piece. You know where I got it?"

"No, where?"

"Right here! About twenty years ago I was plowin' out north of the barn when I ran right over it . . . made the damndest noise, a big thud. Tore hell out of my disk. It's kinda my favorite 'cause of that. Petrified wood from right out back of the barn."

We went over to behold it. It looked like it might have been a trunk or a big limb once. I tried budging it. It was the size of a football and heavy. It had grain markings like I'd seen in museums. We scrutinized it closely.

"This sure is a dandy," I remarked.

"I fancy it 'cause of the markings," said John. "Look at them markings! And to think it was wood once. I like rocks, do you?"

"If they've got a story behind them."

"This one sure does," laughed John. "You ever thought about collectin' rocks?"

"Well, I collect about anything when I get lost."

John laughed again. "I tell ya what," he said, "since you're lost now, here's a proposition for ya. How would you like to have this piece of petrified wood for your own?"

I stared at him, surprised.

"I've always wanted to pass it on to somebody who'd appreciate it. Now, you look like that sort. It's yours if you want it."

John's expression was warm and serious.

"I'd be proud to put it in my collection if you really want me to have it," I replied. "But are you sure? It would put a big empty spot in your garden, and it is a museum piece."

"I'm sure," he said. "It needs a new home!"

We pried it up. I lifted it and dusted it off while John knocked the dirt and the roly-polies off the bottom. We examined it carefully once more, and again I asked, "Are you sure you want me to have it?"

"Yep, it's compliments of John Harbison."

I had misgivings. I wanted him to keep it, but there was no way. He got bubbly about it. I didn't dare say no. He was being bighearted, and that was the issue. He was practicing the goodness of giving. John Harbison is a giver. He does good deeds. Generosity is his trademark. There's a moral behind our rock: 'tis better to give.

Now that that was settled, John kept on being generous. He invited me to stay and sit at his table for supper. "It wouldn't be fancy," he said, "but it would be filling."

I thanked him but passed. It was time to get on my way, and it was still too hot to eat. I departed with an open invitation to come back any time. "Just don't get lost," he kidded, "I've takin' a likin' to ya."

I loaded up the rock and the big jug of water. John wiped his forehead and gave me another crackling smile. "Give it a good home now!"

I waved and took off. I looked over at the water and my rock on the seat. The water would be gone in an hour, but the rock would be with me forever. It would have a new home.

On my way home I thought about how it will soon sit on my patio to mark this experience. It will be among the other things given to me when I've gotten lost. It will rank up there high, right alongside my stone post, arrowhead, pheasant feathers, rattler, barbwire, and a bunch of other rocks.

But what will rank higher than anything is the spirit of John's generosity. It is something to savor *and* pass along.

Me and the Rock

Danny Clark

Bennie Unruh

BENNIE UNRUH

Journal Entry: Aulne, Kansas, 4/12/81

I learned about Bennie Unruh at the store. In the flour section. I saw this plain sack that said: "Unruh's Whole Wheat Flour, Organically Grown, RR 1, Aulne, Kansas." I bought the flour and went looking for my map. Where was Aulne? And who's this Unruh?

Aulne is but a dot on the map, but I found it and Bennie, too. He lives on Main Street. I located him in his garden. He was sprinkling "Bennie Unruh Pesticide" on his rhubarb. I took one look at him and saw vigor. Bennie Unruh is the picture of health.

"What are you sprinkling there?" I asked.

"My own brand of pesticide. It's deadly on little critters."

"What's it made of?"

"Two ingredients," he declared. "Bleached flour and sugar. It's the best combination I've found. It kills 'em a slow, sure death."

"That's what we eat!"

"I know," he said, "and we oughta stop!"

"You look healthy," I said.

"I don't eat bleached flour and sugar," he boasted.

"I didn't figure you did."

"Now, I ain't one of them health nuts either, but I know the way we live now is killing us. We process everything. We need to change and eat like they did years ago. Fresh-grown things. Whole wheat. Real food. I've been doin' it. Look at me."

"How do you keep in shape?"

"I stay active," he reported. "I work. My flour business keeps me busy. I'm a one-man operation. I grow my own wheat. With no chemicals. I irrigate. I store my wheat myself. I mill it, sack it, and take it to the stores. Outside of harvest, I'm a one-man operation.

"People ask me the secret to my flour and vegetables. It makes me laugh. They think I got some secret formula. There ain't no secret. There's just hard work. You gotta give effort. That's what makes your garden grow.

"I learned to farm by the 'Armstrong Method.' That's *Arm-Strong.* Said backwards, that's *Strong-Arm.* You get the picture? I made it 'cause I got up early and I used my arms. I've worked hard all along, ever since I migrated here from Russia as a kid. I was taught that laziness didn't cut it. I can tell ya, nowadays, we don't use our arms. We've gotten fat. The conveniences are killing us. I vowed a long time ago that's not what's gonna kill me. Not conveniences, no sir!

"Look at my garden," he went on. "No secret to it. It takes care. I need to weed it right now. I can't let it go. You gotta weed your garden, no matter who you are."

43

Bennie winked, looked at me, and waited.

"I take it that means you don't get something for nothing."

"That's right," he answered. "You're catching on. Good things come out of hard work. Good crops, good vegetables, a good night's sleep, peace of mind, and another tomorrow. You can't beat that. Hard work is good for ya!"

I winked back at Bennie. "You ought to know," I said. "I bet you live to be 100."

Garden Ground

Ham Keller

Whiteback Buffalo

ROLLING THUNDER

Journal Entry: Canton, 1/19/83

*T*hey are magnificent things, more magnificent than I ever imagined. Standing in this pasture with the cold snow biting at my face, I got chills, the chills of excitement, from seeing real buffalo in the wild grasses and not caged behind chain link fences.

I was finally among them, thanks to Verle Warner, and he let me get close and judge them for myself. Buffalo in their own element look invincible. Creation endowed them with nearly perfect apparatus to survive extremes. Agile, temperamental, and unpredictable, they would still roam the plains in vast herds if they could have only outrun the great white hunters and their big lead bullets.

History states that if you had crossed the plains in 1850 you would have seen the buffalo roaming in mighty black waves that extended for miles. But by the early 1900s they were reduced to sparse herds. Out of ignorance and greed we slaughtered the buffalo unmercifully. We came within an eyelash of

46

making them extinct. Seeing them this close, with the cold northerly blowing in their faces and the white snow collecting on their backs, I saw that they fit in perfectly here—and I didn't! They've been on this continent a million years, adapting, and I haven't! What an outrage!

Back in the pasture, Verle let me get out of the truck. "But don't wander too far," he cautioned. "They're unpredictable things!" I lost track of Verle's advice and got to wandering anyway. One of them turned on me, and I jumped straight-up, truck high! Verle scolded me and said, "Watch out now, that's a two-ton bull you're crossin'!" I got back within an arm's length of the truck, and Verle laughed. He could see I learned my lesson on that one—boy, did I!

Later on, when Verle was good and warm, I told him I wanted a portrait of the herd on the hoof. "Do you think we could get them to run?" I asked. Verle looked at me puzzled, then contemplated the situation. "OK," he muttered. "There's only one thing that's gonna get 'em to move today. Come on and follow me."

We went to the shed, and he pointed to some sacks. "This is what'll make 'em move." I read out loud, "Buffalo Pellets, Purina Buffalo Pellets." "You're kidding," I said, "I didn't even know they made these things." Verle grinned, "Yeah, if you wanna see these babies run, we gotta depend on chow."

So Verle put me in the back of the truck with the pellets, and I let them trickle out while he drove 15 miles per hour across the pasture with the wind coming hard and the snow blowing everywhere. It was a wild ride, but it worked. The buffalo chased us like kids after candy. It was some sight.

Even bouncing and shivering in the back of the truck, my imagination soared. I envisioned buffalo, Indians, the wild wild West, I went into reverie.

I saw myself back in time, back when the West was won. I was a pioneer scout, blazing a trail across these rugged plains. It was the dead of winter, and I was cold and ravenous. Riding west, near an outcrop, I came upon one of the great buffalo herds. Carefully, I followed them. I needed to eat. I would take one for food.

I moved along with them, staying downwind, stalking a straggler. At the right moment, I moved in close. I was about to take aim when, all of a sudden, the wind changed and they caught my scent. The mighty herd panicked, turned on me, and charged. I looked to escape, but it was too late. There was no way out. I was doomed!

I came to and shivered. I realized that really happened back then—what a way to go!

Back again, moving across the pasture, the scene was more exhilarating. They kept coming. It was amazing to see them charge, even if it were for pellets. They are more than agile: they are graceful and quick. When they move in unison, the ground quakes and a thunderous sound is created that is unique in the annals of our past.

Buffalo Head

A roar only the pioneers and the Indians ever knew about. The sound they called "Rolling Thunder"! And here, for this one time, I was getting a gritty sample of it. That very roar: Rolling Thunder!

When it was time to leave for home, I thanked Verle for his patience, his pellets, and the great ride across the pasture. Then I handed him a pint of 80 proof. "Here, Verle, this oughta warm you up."

"Yeah, it had," he grinned.

"My pleasure."

"And you know," he said, "even if it's in a blizzard like today, ain't it kinda nice to see them babies somewhere besides on a nickel?"

"Without a doubt, Verle!—without a doubt!"

Rolling Thunder

Peace Pageant Indian, *Medicine Lodge*

Konza Prairie

CARRY NATION

Journal Entry: Medicine Lodge, Kansas, 4/14/82

The Carry Nation Museum is a little white house in Medicine Lodge. The operators live in back. I arrived before it opened, so I took it upon myself to request an early tour. Frances Heath, the curator, didn't mind. Standing there in her robe, hair net, and thongs, she said, "I'd be happy to show you around, as soon as Carl gets done milking the goat and I get him his breakfast."

After a short wait, Carl came in. At his insistence, I joined him for goat's milk and breakfast. Then Frances, still clad in robe and thongs, gave me the red-carpet tour, complete with full narration. "Carry Nation," she said from memory, "lived here in Medicine Lodge thirteen years, and she intended to close the saloons to save the nation's soul! Carry was very religious, you know. This hatchet here, according to the ones who gave it to us, is the very one Carry used to chop up the bars and wreak her wrath on the sinful."

I brought out my journal and showed Frances a little history about Carry.

Carry Nation was a temperance advocate who set out on a mission.

Carry's alcoholic husband and a broken marriage prompted her to a career in "saloon smashing in Kansas." With hymn-singing women behind her, or alone, she would march into a saloon, sing, pray, hurl vituperations at all "rummies" present and smash fixtures and the stock with hatchets. This crusade, most violent at the turn of the century, led to scattered temporary effects on law enforcement. Carry Nation called the period the "hatchetation of joints" and felt it was the will of the Almighty.

"That's accurate," said Frances. ... Can you imagine her comin' through the door of one of them saloons, then startin' her 'hatchetation'? Here, let me show you her picture."

Looming omnipotent on the museum wall was this big, buxom, strong-willed woman. She looked ready for a fight. "That's her," said Frances, "the one and only Carry Nation."

"I bet she scared the hell out of the 'rummies.' "

"I know one thing," said Frances. "I wouldn't wanna be in the way of her when she was slingin' this here hatchet I'm a holdin'. I'll bet she got a few of them 'rummies' to hop on the wagon out of fright, if nothin' else. She did some convertin', no doubt, but it was a big job. That kind of work will never be done."

"You're right, Frances. If we let history be the judge, Carry missed at saving the nation's soul; but her fervent effort against alcohol on behalf of the holy has leftover effects to this day. In Kansas, it is still a nightmare to consume alcohol and be 'sinful.' "

Francis Heath and Carry Nation

Dude Kolling

THE POWER

Journal Entry: South of the Smoky Hill, 5/20/83

*I*t was hot and dry in Abilene so naturally the topic of the day was water. At the grain elevator I asked if there was anybody who still looked for it. "Yeah, there's an ol' boy down by the Smoky Hill River who still does it. Dude Kolling, he still witches with a stick. Go see him."

Dude Kolling's place is on the river bottomland south of Abilene. I found Dude where he does his day-to-day business, out in the shack where he sells his vegetables. He was in the breezeway, busy, as he put it, "sortin' taters." "Hello," we said to each other as he gave me a strong handshake and a quick smile.

There was electricity. I go on first impressions, and I get a lot out of a strong handshake and a quick smile. They tell me something. Something about grit. In this case, I recognized right away, Dude Kolling was a good one. Before our greeting, I fully intended to devote only the morning to Dude and then get on my way. But, due to a certain spark between us, I stayed 'til dark. Dude's got a manner that can absorb you. The breezeway of his vegetable shack is a gathering place. People come to get vegetables and visit. This whole day, no one who came left right away. No, with Dude, you sit and visit. This stodgy little character has the smile of a child and the voice of a poet. His soft country drawl carries a conversation like a lullaby.

People came and went all day. As Dude counted the day's take on vegetables, I finally said to him, "Dude, do you know why I'm here?"

"Vegetables and a visit, I reckon."

"No," I said, "it's witching. They told me you could find water with a stick."

"I can," he smiled.

"Would you do it for me? I want to see it work."

"Be glad to."

Dude put the day's take in a cigar box and handed it to me. "Hold onto this while I get me a stick." Dude went over to the big willow tree in the yard and fixed himself a Y-shaped branch. "Now, I got water that runs underground through my property. We'll go over to it, and I'll walk over a vein so you get an idea of how I dowse."

We went out a ways from the shack, and Dude said, "You ready? Watch when I hit . . . right about here. Watch the stick." He backed up and walked slowly with the willow branch right in front of him, tightly gripped and pointing up. He walked about four paces and the willow stick moved. It quivered. On the very next step, it plunged forward and pointed right to the ground. "There's water right here," he hollered, "see the stick quiver!"

It was moving all right. I could see it plain as day. A chill shot through me. I didn't expect such dramatics!

"Here, you try it," he coaxed me. "Maybe you got 'the power.' " I took the stick, gripped it hard like Dude and walked slowly right over the vein. Nothing happened. "You ain't got it," he said, shaking his head.

"I don't understand it," said Dude. "It's a power very few of us got. Why me? There's nothing special about me except this. I don't know why I can dowse. It's a funny thing, 'the power.' I believe it's a gift God gives some folks. I was at a family gatherin' when I learned I had it. I was still pretty young and it was at our reunion. Talk got on about a passed-on relative who could dowse. Well, a bunch of us got to tryin' it and with me it worked. I got the willa' branch to point down to the ground. It's quite a feelin'. It's gotta be a gift.

"Now, I don't make a big deal about it, but word gets around. I use it to help folks. Help 'em put in a well. The only chargin' I do is for expenses when I gotta travel a ways. A feller's comin' to get me next week. He's wantin' to put a well on his place. I won't charge him since he's furnishin' the transportation. I just wanta use 'the power' to help him out."

Dude stood quiet for a minute looking at me. Then, out of the clear blue, he said, "How'd you like to feel 'the power'? Let's walk this vein together." My eyes lit up. "Will it work?" "Come on." We went over to the spot where the vein was, and Dude got right behind me. I took the willow branch, and he put his arms under mine. He grappled onto my hands and squeezed like a vise. I walked and he shadowed me. We got to the spot right over the vein, and I felt this quivering in my hands. There were vibrations! The stick was wavering. On the very next step, the willow branch tugged, hurtled forward, and pointed right down at the ground. I couldn't believe it. I felt "the power."

Heck, I pondered. I've been to college. I know the scientific method, but this defied that. Goodbye, skepticism. As sure I was alive and standing there, it happened. There is "the power." Dude's got it and I felt it. He made a believer out of me.

I stood there gaping while Dude laughed. "You didn't believe it, did you?"

"No," I replied, "not until now."

"Never underestimate the power of things you can't see!" he said. "Never underestimate 'the power'!"

Dude's Shack

Ike Morrison

IKE'S TIME

Journal Entry: Kanopolis, Kansas, 11/1/82

I didn't just happen upon Ike Morrison, I was looking for him. I was stuck in a ditch seven miles south of Kanopolis, and he might prove to be my deliverance.

According to the little old lady in a blue Falcon, Ike had this thing-am-a-jig he hooks to his truck and tows with. "Ain't no real tow trucks around here," she said. "Now, Ike, he'd be your only hope in these parts."

I was needing more than hope.

What happened was this. Because I was in a hurry, I picked a new route north, a backroad shortcut. South of Kanopolis in some river bottomland, the road turned to sand. I was cutting down my speed when I saw something in the field to the west of me. I took my eye off the road and came into this S-curve unprepared. I swerved, slid, and landed in a ditch. No damage, but Nadean and I were high centered and stuck. I got out, kicked the ground, and started walking.

That's when the little old lady in the Falcon came along. She rescued me. "Go ahead and cuss," she said. "I do. You ain't the first that's got bit by that S-curve."

When we got to Kanopolis, I thanked her and she dropped me off. "Ike's place," she instructed, "is three blocks south and two west. Look for the thing-am-a-jig in the backyard."

Three blocks south and two west I found the thing-am-a-jig, but not Ike. Naturally, he wasn't home. His neighbor told me he was two blocks east and one north, minding his junk. Ike, he told me, had a salvage yard.

I went there and had to look real hard, but I found him. Right among the many rusted implements was my deliverance. Ike was leaning up against a Minneapolis Moline chassis real comfortablelike, smoking a roll-your-own Bull Durham, watching the grass burn. If I hadn't seen the smoke, I would have walked right past him. His features were that nondescript. He barely moved. And with his complexion the color of rust, he was like a chameleon. He blended right in.

When he saw me, he took a drag off his cigarette and waved casual-like. That spelled him out. He had a looseness. Ike Morrison was slow, deliberate, and highly relaxed. I went up to him.

"Hello, Ike, I'm stuck in a ditch a few miles south of town. Can you pull me out?"

"Yeah," he said, drooling on his Bull Durham, "but I gotta let the fire burn out. It'll take a while. You got some time?"

"I reckon," I replied. "You're my only hope!"

I knew it. First fires, relaxing, then ditches and the helpless—that's how he ranked us. My being stuck wasn't going to hurry him. Not Ike. For the time being, we were stuck, me and everything I owned. I took a deep breath, sighed, leaned up against the chassis and started watching the grass burn. I was on Ike's time.

Some umpteen Bull Durhams later, the grass burned out. Ike moved and I jumped for joy. We got the thing-am-a-jig and headed south to what everybody calls "the darndest curve in the county." Ike declared (in what I judged the height of his emotion), "That curve is terrible! I maintain they oughta straighten it or put a sign on it!" That statement got my adrenalin pumping.

At the "darndest curve in the county" I got a shock. There at the ditch, inspecting my predicament, was half the town. Ike laughed, "You don't need me, you got volunteers!"

Yes, indeed, the Kanopolis Volunteer Army was ready and able. No thing-am-a-jig, just hands. One, two, three, and they heave-hoed Nadean right out of the ditch. Ike and I just watched. What comfort I felt. Good Samaritans still live among us.

Uplifted and grateful, I thanked the volunteers for their good deed. Then I handed Ike something for his trouble. Something he didn't want. I had to force it on him. He doesn't like to accept things unearned. But I explained to him it was a reward. A reward for teaching me a lesson: how to be more relaxed!

Those of us in a hurry ought to hang around guys like Ike. We'd see more clearly that hurrying has its hazards.

Country Corner

Jerry Holmes, *Alliance, Nebraska*

A Dying Breed

Journal Entry: Alliance, Nebraska, 6/12/83

On Box Butte Avenue in Alliance, I spent this Saturday afternoon in an empty chair listening to Jerry Holmes give his eulogy to "a dying breed." That's what he calls himself and other barbers like him.

"This building's been here since 1912, and I've been in it since 1954," he bragged. "It's seen a lot of haircuts but let me tell ya, it ain't what it used to be.

"I remember when this shop of mine was packed on Saturdays. I used to cut hair 'til my hands got cramps. It used to be that every man and boy in Alliance got their hair cut on Box Butte Avenue on Saturdays. In the heyday, this place was hoppin'. Every chair had a barber. These here benches you see empty now, they were packed. I had a shoeshine boy. We gave shaves, sold tonic and butch wax, and cut late. Geez, did we cut late! Look around you now, this is a typical Saturday these days—nothin'! I swear, I never imagined it'd come to this!

"I graduated from Omaha Barber College in 1936, and I've kept track. Out of a class of seventy-five, there's just three of us left cuttin', and, believe it or not, all three of us are right here in Alliance.

"The big change came in 1968. That's when long hair came in. It's been downhill ever since. Long hair, weird fads. I'd shout hallelujah if flattops ever come back in . . . but that's wishin'!

"It's a fact, good ol' barbers have gone by the wayside. We're a dying breed! When I sweep the shop now, it's not 'cause there's hair on the floor. I sweep because most of the time there's nothin' to do. You could eat off this floor. Make note, you're lookin' at a dying breed!"

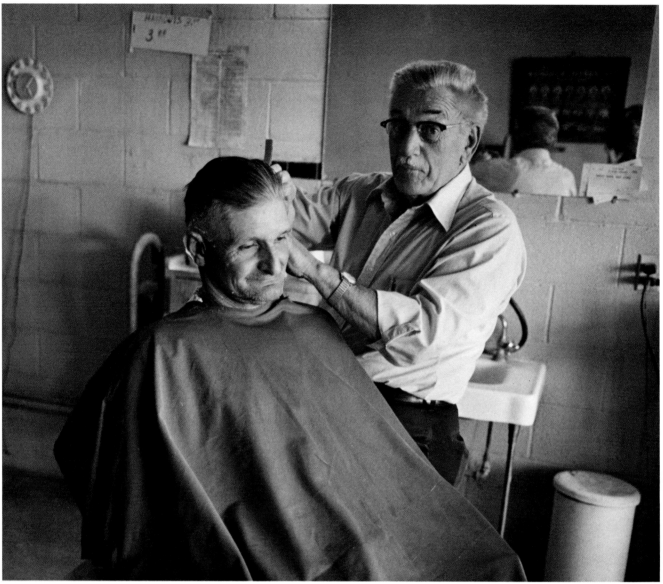

Merle Hooker's Haircut, Merle Hooker and Carl Ferner

MERLE HOOKER'S HAIRCUT

Journal Entry: Carl Ferner's Barbershop, 9/16/82

THE SCENE:
Four of us were in Carl Ferner's barbershop on Saturday afternoon. Carl had the scissors. Merle Hooker was in the chair. Mel Marsh was waiting his turn. And I, L.A., had just wandered in.

Carl: Merle, what'll it be? The usual?
Merle: Yeah, make it the regular.
L.A.:   Merle, what's the regular?

Merle:	Close on the sides.
L.A.:	How often do you get the regular?
Merle:	About every four months.
Carl:	(Reaching for the scissors) Geez, Merle, is it that seldom? That's only three cuts a year . . . times $3. Let's see, that's $9 a year. Dang, Merle, I oughta fertilize your scalp or raise my price!
Merle:	(Grinning) Now, Carl, don't go and do that. You're high enough!
Mel Marsh:	(Thinking Carl was serious) You get me more than three times a year, Carl. You can raise your price to Merle, but leave me be. I come in once a month, rain or shine!
Carl:	Let me tell ya, you both got it good. Listen to this. My boy had one of them styles in a shop in Salina the other day. Dang thing took $11 out of his pocket, and here's the good part. You can't even tell it. I had to ask him if he had it cut! Eleven dollars for somethin' that didn't look like nothin'. "That's a style," my boy told me. A haircut that don't look like one.
Merle:	(Staring blankly) Eleven dollars for somethin' you can't tell. Ain't no use in that!
Mel Marsh:	This generation of kids is crazy. They throw their money away.
Carl:	(Looking suspiciously at L.A.) How much do you pay for that windblown look?
L.A.:	I'm not telling. You'd die.
Carl:	I'll bet it's a whole year of Merle's haircut money!
Mel Marsh:	And probably more!
L.A.:	You're in the ball park, but I'm still not telling.
Merle:	(Grinning again) My hair grows slow, I'm lucky!
Mel Marsh:	Merle, you get it cut so close, it's a wonder it grows at all.
Carl:	Hold still, Merle. I'm givin' you an outline.
Merle:	(Sits frozen, with the same grin on his face) I'm holdin'.
Mel Marsh:	(Smirking) Hurry up, Carl, maybe we can convince L.A. here to get a trim.
Carl:	You're all done, Merle, pay up.
Merle:	(Pays his $3, looks in the mirror close, grins again) I sure got my money's worth!
Carl:	Now *that's* value!
Mel Marsh:	I want mine short, Carl, but not that short. Don't get the soup bowl out for me!
Carl:	How about you, L.A., you want the bowl?
L.A.:	No way! I'm just observing. When I walk out of here, I still want the wind to blow my hair.
Carl:	You'll regret it!
L.A.:	No, I won't!
Mel Marsh:	Don't you wanna look like Merle?
L.A.:	It's time for me to go. I better get out of here before I get talked into a "trim."

(Carl, Merle, and Mel laugh.)

L.A. walked out and the screen door slammed. He took a few steps, then stopped, turned around, and, smiling, said through the door, "OK, I'll confess. I pay $15 for this windblown look."

Carl, Merle, and Mel stood silent. Their mouths fell open. They stared blankly through the screen door.

Their looks proved it. There will always be a generation gap!

Merle Hooker "My Money's Worth"

Wilson Czech Band

INEZ MARSHALL

Journal Entry: Portis, Kansas, 8/30/82

*P*ortis, Kansas: Population 90
I put on the brakes when I saw the only big sign in Portis. It read: "Continental Sculpture Hall, The Only One Of Its Kind Of The Kind, It's On This Side Of Main Street." From that instant, it got peculiar.

By sheer accident I was about to stumble onto a renowned folk artist and one of the most notoriously original women anywhere. Under that sign was the sculptress, Portis' own Inez Marshall. I learned immediately any time spent with Inez is mystifying. The first thing she said to me after "Who are you?" and "You can't take my picture" was this: "I get inspiration from a voice. A voice speaks to me."

Inez Marshall

"Out loud?" I asked.

"Out loud!" she replied. "When I first touch a piece of stone, I don't even know what I'm gonna create. I stew on it. I wait for the voice. I get inspired. Then it comes. The voice comes . . . Once the voice spoke, 'Inez, there's an eagle in that rock, get it out!' "

A voice! . . . Her frankness threw me. I jogged my memory. Had I ever met someone this candid? No! This could only get more interesting. What would she tell me next?

"My career began on my back," she rambled. "I broke it in the dirty '30s. I was laid up in the hospital, down in the dumps. But then, somebody brought me a rock. It cheered me up. Right then I knew my calling. Stone! I'd be a sculptress. I put the rock on the table by my bed and stared at it. I got inspired. That's when I first heard the voice. Right there in the hospital. It said to me, 'Inez, you will be a sculptress.' "

"Out loud?"

"Out loud!"

Inez, I discovered, is uncanny. She wears cowboy boots, rides motorcycles, and quarries her own stone. Her burly hands and big-boned frame make her manlike, yet her soft raspy voice is feminine. She has intuition. Her temperament is fascinating. There is sincerity in her strangeness. With that far-off look she gets, there must be a voice. She's a wild-eyed original if there ever was one.

Inside the Continental Sculpture Hall I examined her handiwork. There were sculptures galore. Most notable were her full-size statues of Abe Lincoln and his family, a four-foot high, 600-pound, limestone Model T Ford, a miniature limestone hospital and schoolhouse with doctors, nurses, teachers, and children. And there were limestone fish, birds, and animals. What overwhelmed me was the paint. Inez paints everything. All of her sculptures are covered in high gloss enamel. There's something peculiar about painted stone.

When she showed me the huge rock that would eventually be a full-size Harley Davidson, I said, "That's beautiful limestone. Will you paint it like everything else?"

"Sure," she said, "it'll be even more beautiful when it's a Harley Davidson painted black."

"Why do you paint your sculptures, Inez?"

"I like 'em authentic. It gives 'em a touch, realness! See here, look at this rainbow trout. I even put the speckles on its belly. Ain't it pretty?"

"Oh yes," I said, going with the flow.

This tour was a topper. Every expression was original. Every detail was strange. The voice, the inspiration, the far-off looks, they were part of it. There was this energy. With Inez leading the way, this was not just a tour, this was an encounter. At her bright red limestone guitar we stopped.

"This here's a genuine stone Fender guitar!"

"What does that thing weigh?"

"Over 100 pounds. I want you to do something," she instructed. "Get up there close to that guitar and pluck them strings . . . You ever felt a stone guitar vibrate? This one here does. Put your hand right above them strings and pluck. Did you feel it? My stone guitar vibrates.

"Now, stand back and listen. I'll pluck . . . Hear that? It twangs. Did you ever hear a stone guitar twang like that before? Not many know it, but stone twangs. The sound that comes out of that thing even surprises me. It twangs like a wood one . . . That's the mystery of my work. I never know 'til I hear the voice or I get to the end."

She was going strong now. I plucked, she talked, and the guitar twanged. I watched her. What was next?

The twanging must have set her off because suddenly she got quiet. Her expression changed. She appeared to look through me, somewhere far-off. She pulled out an old pocket watch. "Tour's over," she huffed. "I just got inspired!" She walked to the back of the Sculpture Hall and disappeared. I stood there in silence, dazed. The lack of her presence was eerie. I put my dollar in the box and left.

69

I moved across Main Street and sat on the curb, mesmerized. I reread the sign, "The Only One Of Its Kind, . . . On This Side Of Main Street." Portis was empty. I tried to gather myself, but I couldn't move.

I was sitting there looking at the sign, letting it soak in, when, no kidding, I thought I heard a voice. Out loud it said to me, "What did you think of my sculptress?" I shook my head and muttered, "She's one of a kind."

Lester Stroede

MELVIN HOSS
THE MAN BORN DIFFERENT

Journal Entry: Kanopolis, 6/4/82

*T*hat's him by the garage. He's over there with the groom."
"That's Melvin Hoss?"
"Yep, in the flesh and blood, that's him, Wild Man Melvin."
I went over by the garage. "So you're Melvin Hoss?" I said to him.
"Was yesterday, am today, and will be tomorrow . . . What's the deal?

Melvin Hoss and the Groom

You got a gripe?"

"No."

"Then here, have a good swig of my Double-Trouble 7-Up. It'll put ya in the mood for a weddin'."

I took a swig of Double-Trouble, and it burned a fiery path straight to my stomach. A big grin broke over Melvin Hoss' face. I caught the wild glare in his eyes, and I realized there was a whole lot of trouble right here by the garage.

It was at Stroede's Place where I first heard about Melvin Hoss. Stroede's is unique in its own right. It's a combination filling station, pool hall, and gathering spot in Kanopolis. It's the only place I've ever been where, under one roof, you can eat, drink, visit, play pool, and watch your tire being fixed, all at the same time.

Another distinguishing feature of Stroede's is the sound. In Stroede's there's this constant conglomeration of racket, always amplified to pandemonium. Most any time, you can hear tires hissing, pool balls banging, the jukebox blaring, and somebody's always yelling. Over the noise one day I heard about Melvin. Somebody was hollering, bragging real loud about notorious types, and that led straight to him. Above the noise, I was informed of Melvin's general nature.

"Melvin Hoss, they broke the mold with him. For plain orneriness, he's one of a kind. Melvin don't candycoat nothin'. He tells it like it is."

"Melvin's all vinegar. You don't tiptoe around him, you kick and stomp. You want Melvin with ya in a brawl. If he's in a fight, it ends up a knockdown dragout. He don't back down from nothin'."

"It's simple, Melvin Hoss was born different!"

Over by the gargage, staring at him up close, I saw it. He was "born different." His wild look had permanence. While everyone waited for the wedding to begin, Melvin had the groom cornered as if it were just before his execution. He was forcing him to take extra swigs of his Double-Trouble. He said it was the least he could do for his buddy on "doomsday." Get him smashed! Melvin made me and everybody over by the garage take more swigs of his Double-Trouble, too.

"What's in that?" I asked him.

"95 percent vodka!"

"Whew!"

Something was bound to happen. I could see it in his grin. Melvin was like a firecracker ready to be lit. Sooner or later he would go off. It was sooner.

During the backyard wedding, he did the unthinkable. When it was time for the ceremony to begin, somebody hollered, "Places, everybody," and we all went over to the patio. Somehow I ended up right next to Melvin, row two, seat three. It was the usual backyard wedding, semi-formal and 100 percent down-home. Things were going fine until the justice of the peace said,

"If there is anyone here who has cause to object to this holy union of matrimony, let him speak or forever hold his peace."

There was a slight pause; then Melvin did it. He objected. Loud and clear, he blurted out, "I object!" Momentarily there was dead silence. My mouth fell open in disbelief. I cringed from the impact of such an outburst. I glanced at Melvin. I couldn't believe it. He looked proud. I was sitting right next to the only person I had ever met who objected to the holy union of matrimony.

I figured this was it, we'd be run off and arrested, the whole second row. I was holding my breath. But when I finally looked around, I was dumbstruck. There was no shock. No one paid one bit of attention to Melvin, not the bride, not the groom, not the justice of the peace, not anyone. The ceremony just went on without a hitch. Somehow it must have been known that he might do it. Heck, he's probably done it before. I saw it on all the faces, "Melvin, he's liable to do anything!"

The wedding ended with the kiss, the march, and many congratulations. The bride threw the bouquet, and afterward no one even mentioned "the incident." As we walked over to the dance hall for the reception, Melvin reloaded his 7-Up bottle, and I asked him why he objected to the holy union of matrimony. Without hesitation he said. "I'm one of them fellers who's gotta speak his mind. I come right out with what I got on my chest. Weddin's don't stop me. I tell it like it is.

"Another thing, that was my buddy up there, and I owed it to him. Wait 'til he gets a few knots on his head. Take it from a man who knows the rougher side of cohabitatin'. Cohabitatin' ain't what it's cracked up to be. Every man oughta have warnin', especially a buddy. That's why I spoke up. It was legal. The judge gave me the chance. I had to do it."

Melvin passed around the bottle again, and there was tingling being felt. "Mr. Pho-nog-ra-pher," he slurred, "weddin's ain't half bad once the cera-mony is over. What ya say we hang a left here in this dance hall and raise some holy hell. You can get a pit-chur of me stompin' on the hardwood. Tonight I'm gonna get wild!"

In the dance hall he kept his word. When he hit the hardwood, everyone backed off and he stomped up a storm. For better or worse, this was going to end up being one hell of a night. My head was already pounding from the Double-Trouble, but I didn't mind. Melvin made up for the pain. I had developed an instant affection for him. He might be rough around the edges, but you can't beat him for his outright spontaneity. He's as candid as they come. If all of us were as honest and brash as Melvin, there would be a lot less, as he put it, "bullshit bein' blown around!"

"That's what you gotta admire about Melvin," said a buddy, "he don't care what the neighbors think. He was born different!"

Melvin Hoss on Saturday

LESTER STRAILY

Journal Entry: Kanopolis, 9/5/82

*L*ester Straily lives in a cave," folks said, so I went for a look. They were wrong. Lester lives near some caves. His home is actually a storm cellar. He's there for a reason, he told me . . . the government!

"They burnt me once," he said. "They burnt me real good. I'll be damned if I let 'em do it again. They can't 'doze down a cellar."

"What did they do?"

"They run me off my place to put in the reservoir. Oh, they paid me, but money ain't land. They made the Straily place a reservoir!

"That soured me. Takin' a man's land would sour anybody. I don't trust 'em now, not the government. I don't trust 'em any further than I can throw 'em. They ain't runnin' me outta here, I tell ya. I'm underground!"

Lester Straily has a callus in a sensitive spot. He gets rubbed wrong anytime anyone mentions the reservoir or the old place or the government. Standing in his cellar, I found myself siding with him. On his turf, he can be convincing.

Looking at his gruff exterior, I found him to be calloused all over. Outwardly, he's rough-edged and haggard. He has a thick hide. His hard blue eyes are worn and faded. You could light a match on his emery cloth face. Living hard and thinking hard have toughened him. That's the price he's paid for his independence.

Lester exists simply. In his cellar he's got electricity and a hot plate. He used to have a TV. There's a dangling light bulb, some newspapers, a stack of books, a little food, and a few pictures. He has one roommate, a bull snake that comes and goes. "I don't mind him," said Lester. "Me and that snake, we give each other room!"

"It's cozy," I said.

"It's shelter," he replied. "Storm proof and it stays about the same temperature all year-round. If you like bein' your own man, you don't need more."

Being independent, that's what marks Lester. That's how he got labeled "cave man." Because he's a recluse, some folks have kept their distance. Lester may be a recluse, but he's not strange. I sized him up quickly. He's got all his marbles. He's not even a hermit. He goes to town, does business, and talks to folks who've taken the time to know him. If anything, Lester's a survivor of another age. He would have fit in perfect homesteading a dugout 100 years ago. Lester is still three-fourths frontiersman!

"I believe a man don't need much," he declared. "People are fools for always wantin' the way they do. The more they got, the more they want. It's crazy . . . wantin' keeps 'em from thinkin' . . . from bein' sensible. They want to get big and rich, and that's what's wrong with us. That's what happened to the

Lester Straily

government. It got big."

"Speaking of big, Lester, they told me in town you grow some pretty big watermelons. They said your patch is the best in Ellsworth County. Is that so?"

"Well," he smiled all out. "Now, you're talking. Melons are my kind of subject."

I did it. I'd found Lester's soft spot. I knew he had one. Melons!

"I heard watermelons take a knack. Tell me how you do it?"

"It's like this," he said as his whole tone of voice softened up, childlike, "watermelons take to my sandy soil, that's luck. But I plant when the time is right, that's common sense. I get 'em all in the ground when the time's right. Plantin' is crucial for good melons. When I plant, I get fired up. I go like there ain't no tomorrow. I go to plantin' with a full head of steam!"

"A full head of steam?"

"Yeah," he pointed as he spoke, "a tuned up Rototiller, a fresh lit stogy, and a couple swigs off some good Jim Beam. That's a full head of steam. That's what gets me goin' like there ain't no tomorrow!"

I pointed at the mound of Jim Beam bottles over in the ditch. "That's a lot of plantin'."

Lester's hard blue eyes lit up. "Yeah, it is, but you gotta keep rust outta your pipes, too. Jim Beam's got many uses. I use the steam it gives for insulation in the winter. Antifreeze! That mound of bottles covers all year-round!"

We laughed, and Lester said, "One man's sin is another man's steam!"

"When's watermelon time?" I asked him. "I want to come back and try one."

"You're welcome back any time. I'll pick out a good melon and keep it for ya."

"In the cellar?"

"Yeah," Lester sang, "in the cellar . . . my home sweet home!"

Lester's Home Sweet Home

Jirak Brothers

Miss Liberty

MISS LIBERTY

Journal Entry: Smith Center, Kansas, 10/22/84

I was rambling up 281 on my way to another monument when I spotted her, a genuine replica of the thing we cherish the most: Miss Liberty.

Perched atop a roadside grade, she was weathered, worn, and bullet-ridden but, nevertheless, still radiant and shining brightly this uncommonly tranquil morning. At her base I read where she was erected by the Boy Scouts in 1954 as a pledge of fidelity and dedicated "to our forefathers who made possible the freedom of these United States."

Taken aback by the view and touched by her radiance, this was a time for me to ponder *liberty.* So I drew on my history and dwelt on her past as our symbol of opportunity. I paused—and then had to view her with newfound respect. I walked around her and climbed up beside her to see what she could see. Below her was America and the beautiful fruited plain. I had to look again, so I got in my van and pulled up close to the pedestal of stone she sits on. Then I got out and climbed up on the roof where we could both see this sight together. America and this prairie, in all their open splendor.

This was an invigorating morning. The kind you must give respect. There was a light frost glittering on the ground. The air was raw and clean. And the prairie scent was pungent. And, for some reason, it was especially quiet. Nothing moved in this "hour of the pearl." There was not a single soul around.

It was then, right on the top of my van, that something stirred me. A feeling I can't quite describe. It was staggering . . . Up high above this plain, next to Miss Liberty, I felt independent, patriotic, and free, as I had never felt before. There was this strong emotion, and it wanted to burst out. I had to express it . . . so, without further thinking, I stood up, put my hand on her torch, and belted out "America The Beautiful" at the top of my lungs! It was a natural-born reflex . . . and the lyrics just flowed. "Oh spacious skies" never sounded so good nor had more meaning! It just came up from somewhere inside me. And I felt it in every pore. Here was a genuine American moment: for me, Miss Liberty, and those forefathers who made this all possible.

More rare, here was a moment I didn't think about restraint. I let the surge of patriotism pick me up and carry me away. I was "out there," feeling what the immigrants must have felt when they first put their feet on this soil, and I didn't give a hoot, either, that someone might see me. Some lunatic standing on top of a van next to a miniature Statue of Liberty in the middle of nowhere, waving his arms and screaming at the top of his lungs. Heck, let 'em think I'm crazy. I'm not holding back. Not this time. Let the walls come down—I may never get a chance like this again.

You see, those immigrants who came here and this statue I was next to, they meant something to me. And, because of them and this moment of realization, I got all choked up inside. I nearly cried.

Oh hell! Who am I kidding? I cried a little. Grown men can cry . . . this is America . . . and we still have a dream . . . and I never want to forget it.

There's nothing on earth like freedom!

Chimney Rock

Patriotism, Memorial Day, *Hunter*

PATRIOTISM

Journal Entry: Hunter, Memorial Day, 1983

Memorial Day is a unique holiday in small towns. It still has a lot of meaning. People come out and have fellowship. They pay their respects. There's not much to distract them. They have roots in memories. And over their shoulders, they live with the past. You can feel the connection among them on this day. It's the patriotism.

I'm in Hunter every Memorial Day. It's my duty. They expect me there, and I wouldn't miss it. Their own brand of coming-together is simple and down-home. It starts early. People gather at the cemetery to put down flowers, look at graves, and remember names. Then, around nine o'clock, the people line up, and the American Legion color guard marches from the main road into the cemetery with flags and salutes. Everyone stands at attention while the cemetery flag is raised half-mast. Then the preacher reads a bible verse from Psalms. A prayer is said for the dead, especially for those who lost their lives in the service of their country. On command, while the crowd is hushed, the color guard fires their rifles into the sky. Then a lone trumpeter plays taps. There is a whole minute of silence. Then the color guard marches out among the people who stand again and salute. A simple and solemn affair but, underneath, there's more to it than that.

My official position on Memorial Day is chauffeur. I drive the color guard between cemeteries and just around. We load up and go in my van or in Delmer Gier's big Pontiac. Chauffeur is a position I'm proud of. It puts me right in the thick of things. During the drives we partake in our annual ritual. We acknowledge the day, then we celebrate having a holiday together. We take a hoot off the pint being passed around, and we potshot the wild blue yonder with the Legion rifles. It's a tradition. The riding around is a good time for camaraderie. No chores, no business, just stories and catching up. We cut loose a little. Even hard-working farmers have got to have some time to cut loose. And that's the other side of it. Memorial Day is a good time.

I never miss Memorial Day because of the camaraderie, but there's another reason it's an annual affair for me. I call it "the joy of down-home observation." I relish the little things that make Memorial Day in Hunter unique. The way things are carried out is worth noticing. The official parts are unadorned and just one cut above the ordinary. There is a lack of detail that gets me. Nothing is polished. No part of the ceremony is rehearsed. It just kind of happens. No fancy dress. Uniforms are a little wrinkled. Some of the guns don't fire. Taps is off-key. And everything is slightly out of step. But that's the beauty of it. It's not put on for show. It's honest. And, if there's a lack of detail and refinement, the sincerity still hits home. Memorial Day in Hunter has character. I try to describe it occasionally, but description falls short. You've got to see it to feel its uniqueness. To me, this day is the epitome of the way real life works: just slightly out of step.

This year, just before I lined up the color guard for the annual flag-waving portrait, we had a discussion. There was the usual talk about crops and neighbors and those passed on, but somehow we got beyond the usual. We ended up on patriotism.

"What is patriotism out here?" I asked them. "What's the meaning of it?"

"Well, it ain't the Fourth of July," they told me. "No, it was more than showing your colors one day out of the year. It has deeper meaning than going to cemeteries and standing up for the flag. Patriotism comes from the gut."

"It's how you live your life. Patriotism is being thankful each and every day for what you have and those who gave it to you. You honor it by the way you live."

"I think we're losing track of its meaning," said Bobby Wiles.

All agreed. "Patriotism can be a touchy subject . . . Everybody thinks they got a corner on it. Politicians preach about it. Some people take it for granted. Others ignore it. A lot don't ever think about it. But we farmers," they told me, "we live it . . . That's patriotism!"

Bobby Wiles

Old Glory

Bluff City

BLUFF CITY

*I*t looked like a ghost town at first, Bluff City did. But then I saw the flag and a little sign of life around the post office so I went there to see what thrived in a tidbit town.

Inside were Laverne Marks and Charlotte Berry of the U.S. Postal Service. Laverne is the plump, proud postmaster of Bluff City.

"What thrives here?" I asked.

"We do!" boasted Laverne.

"Bluff City's only had two postmasters the last seventy years, and you're lookin' at one of 'em . . . I've been here since 19 and 45!" he proclaimed. "Bluff City may not look like much, but there's still a few good folks left. I guarantee ya! We held on here, the good bunch, we held on!"

Being talkative and having taken kindly to my inquisitive nature, Laverne came out from behind the old, official rolltop desk and continued by giving me his version of Bluff City "in her heyday."

"When I was a kid, this was quite a town," he bragged. "We used to have a railroad, a grocery and hardware store, a blacksmith's shop, an elevator, a library, and a good barbershop. And there was a dance on Saturday nights. My folks used to have to hunt me down to get me to go to bed. I used to hang out on the sidewalks and take it all in . . . Bluff City was somethin' back then—a community. Then the railroad moved. And that was that. These days all we got are memories. And it's a pity the small towns are fadin' away."

"What's kept you holdin' on?" I asked him.

"It's roots," he uttered. "You are what you're born to . . . and Bluff City ain't bad . . . it's quiet. And we keep up. Why, when I get done here, I can go home, relax, and see the world on TV . . . and that's enough for me: the mail, Bluff City, and the world on TV."

Wallace Champeny, "Oxford's Best"

ABOUT ABILENE

Journal Entry: Abilene, Kansas, 6/28/84

*A*bilene had history. I knew this. But there was some first-person interpretation I wanted, a few more facts with a little more color. I was after these facts early Saturday, before the sun began to have smothering effects and send folks back inside to hibernate near air conditioners.

As luck would have it, nine o'clock on the dot, right on Main Street, I got my interpretation—the exact kind I was looking for. That's where I met Albert Sewell, "Man about Abilene."

Across the street was where I first spotted him—or he spotted me. We both sort of stuck out. The tourist and the "Man about Abilene." Albert Sewell looked dapper in what I judged to be his Sunday morning best. Clinging to him were a pressed blue suit, starched white shirt, a wide yellow bow tie, and a new straw hat, slightly tilted to accommodate the uniqueness that said "just him."

This kind of attire is unusual for a prairie town. And with it, Albert Sewell formed a direct contrast to the usual trapping of jeans, denim shirts, and give-me caps. Somewhat amazed, I sensed that here was a man in a country town on a hot summer morning, dressed to kill and enjoying it. He had it written all over him. Why, he didn't even have sweat on his brow. To stare wide-eyed at Albert Sewell was pure entertainment. Even his movement was alluring. He loped.

So there we were, surveying each other in depth. Then, with long gangling strides, Albert Sewell moved across the street, sauntered up to me, and, with a kind smile and a courteous twang, he asked, "May I help you?" I grinned and said, "Well, maybe. I'm looking for some information about Abilene, its history."

"You came to the right person," he beamed. "What would you like to know?"

Still feasting on his peculiarities, I fumbled for words. I was still saying to myself, "Wow, here is a man who relishes in being different!"

Finally, I asked, "What do you know about Abilene in the pioneer days?"

"Quite a little," he replied confidently. So, at the main intersection, Albert Sewell got on about Abilene.

"Well, I'll tell you," he began, "most of us here in Abilene, we cherish it for its peace and quiet. We've got plenty! But it wasn't always like this. No sir, this was a wide-open cattle town back when the West was won. Back then, Abilene had a reputation!"

"What kind?"

"The worst," he proclaimed.

"It was a boom town. It's where the railroad, the cattle baron, and the cowboy all met. And the effect was dramatic. Because it was the end of the trail,

Albert Sewell

Abilene grew up overnight.

"In those days, when the cowboys got here, they went crazy. They spent the money they got from the cattle barons immediately. And they spent it on things unrighteous. And unrighteous things were readily available. And that's where the reputation comes in.

"Abilene was known for its sin. Sin of all kinds. Back then, sin was a booming business. There were two sides of the tracks: north and south, good and bad. On the south side, the Texas side, the bad side, the saloons, gambling joints, and houses of ill repute flourished! There were shootouts, brawls, and spectacles nightly. The darned place glowed red! It was heaven for the cowboy, but a headache and forbidden ground for the do-gooder.

"It even spilled over across the tracks. They went and got Wild Bill Hickock to clean it up. At that time, he was the most feared man alive. They made him sheriff, and they say he put notches on his belt in the name of law and order, but that still didn't stop it. Believe it or not, Abilene was just like a Hollywood movie, only real!"

Albert and I stared south across the tracks, where once upon a time it all took place. And you wouldn't believe it. Today it's normal. Just a regular neighborhood with a few old buildings. I made a note that the ghosts of sin are long gone in Abilene. It's so quiet you wonder what they do.

"Yes," he shook his head, "it's kinda hard to believe that 100 years ago this little place led the nation in sin. It was time that got to Abilene."

We continued to discuss time, change, and history, but my real pleasure was getting lost in Albert's delivery. With his meticulous cadence, he could sure give voice to a story. There was something special about Albert Sewell. He had poise.

We finished up on what Albert called good history: Abilene's favorite son, Ike Eisenhower. Then he had to go. As he loped away in his own package of colorful characteristics, I jotted down in my journal that besides knowing history, this man, Albert Sewell, had distinction. I admire that.

Down in front of his insurance office, he waved, adjusted his straw hat, and opened the door for one of his clients. I took it in admiringly. On my way out of town, I tried to imagine myself being like Albert Sewell someday, full of history and comfortably dressed to the hilt. Yes, indeed, someday I'd like to be loud without even saying a word.

EARL ARTLEY SPEAKS

Journal Entry: Russell Springs, 6/20/82

*R*ussell Springs is out of the way unless you're wandering out of the way on purpose. It sits cozily on a mound: a courthouse, a main street, some houses, and a few folks. That's the extent of Russell Springs. But the courthouse is a beauty. It's all limestone and one of those they call "a castle on the plains." Earl Artley was locking the door of this castle when I came across the square. I'm glad I stopped him. He's someone who knows a lot about Russell Springs and a little about life.

"Back in the late 1800s this was a hub of a town. Stagecoaches came through here east and west. This was the heart of Indian country, though. It was risky then. The stage line advertised, 'This is the shortest, but most dangerous, route west.'

"I ain't so sure that was a good advertising slogan. The stage line died out, but we. got a good museum. Come on, I'll show you through the courthouse.

"Over here we got the museum. Look at all the arrowheads and the cavalry stuff. Take your time, there's lots to see. Now, over there is the sheriff's office. That room down the hall there, that's where folks pay their taxes. And let's go upstairs. That's my favorite place.

"Here's the courtroom. This place was darn near my second home. I was county attorney for twenty years. I had my office just below on the second floor. I tried many a case right here where I'm standing. All kinds! This room looks empty, but for this fella there's lots of memories.

"In 19 and 38 I ran for county attorney. I won by two votes. I got contested, but I won again on appeal. My salary was $75 a month, and that wasn't bad back then. In fact, it was downright comfortable. I was a greenhorn, too, fresh out of Washburn Law School.

"I got along, but I had a lot to learn. I got my first good advice in law school. A judge, early on, said, 'Earl, you can be a little duck on a big pond, or you can be a big duck on a little pond.'

"Well, I pondered that and chose the latter. That's how I ended up here. The little pond was Russell Springs. And it was the right choice.

"Because of this pond, and its having good ducks on it, I've been lucky. To do it again, I wouldn't change a thing. Being a big duck on a little pond keeps you normal. There's nothin' fancy here. You can't get too big for your britches no matter who you are.

"Being happy here in this little pond says something about the people. They're as big as the land. Good and decent all the way through."

Earl Artley

Jim Nelson, The Counter Check

THE COUNTER-CHECK

Journal Entry: Jewell, Kansas, 10/10/82

J im Nelson did me a favor. He stood in front of the Jewell Bank with what I call the "phenomenon of the plains"—the counter-check.

Jim is a farmer and an artist. I met him at the counter in the Jewell Cafe. He gets his meals there for his painting that hangs on the wall. "It's good ol'-fashioned barter," he told me. "The cafe is earning my painting by letting me get full on good food. You can't beat that. It's something me and the cafe are both happy about. We still do that here: barter!"

"Do you still use these?" I asked him as I reached down the counter, past the syrup and salt, and picked up a stack of counter-checks.

"Oh, yeah," he said, "we use them here. They're handy. They're for people like me. I always forget my checkbook. Explain to me why you call them the 'phenomenon of the plains.' "

"I've been all over," I said, "and the only places I've found counter-checks are in little towns. Out here off the beaten path, I can go into a cafe, a pool hall, or a five and dime and always on the counter, right out in the wide open, are these checks. It astounds me! Checks you can just pick up and write out. These things wouldn't work in regular America. In the cities they would be a nightmare. They would bounce off the walls. It's only out here that they work. That's why they're a phenomenon. They're indicators: evidence that honesty is still a part of small-town life. Banks and shopkeepers still have a little faith, and small-town people still have a little pride. It's sort of sad, but, in this day and age, the best place to find wide open honesty is still right here in little prairie towns like Jewell."

"Folks around here do still care," admitted Jim.

"Knowing this," I said, "I give counter-checks special status. I've got a soft spot for them. I go out of my way to see one being written. For the integrity, I like to gawk. There's a certain body language about a counter-check transaction. There couldn't be a more honest moment. It's a carry-over from what it was like before contracts, auditors, and every man for himself: when people shook hands and gave their word.

"Counter-checks are significant," I concluded. "I even wrote one out once."

"Where?" Jim asked.

"In a small town like Jewell."

"That ought to be good. Tell me that one."

One morning, after a short stack and coffee, I hung around this cafe to eyeball a couple of counter-check transactions. I noticed the waitress right away. She was a gem. She wore all white and had her hair in a bun. Her face was puckered, wrinkled, and covered with thick, powder-brown makeup. She kept an extra pencil tucked up over her ear. She was the hustly-bustly type, constantly moving her feet and her mouth. You should have seen how she could glide between tables with her coffee pot. She was taking orders and giving advice at the same time. She had this all-knowing air about her. The cafe was her domain.

I decided to have fun and test her. I waited for her to get behind the counter; and, while she was busy pulling orders, I strolled up to the cash register, picked up a check off the counter and wrote out a big one for pancakes and coffee. I signed it and handed it over to her, "the unsuspecting waitress." It was hard to keep a straight face.

She looked the check over and then glared at me with her gooseberry gray eyes. "I've been watching you out of the corner of my eye all morning," she said. "If you're Jesse James like this here check says, then I'm Annie Oakley; and if you got a million bucks, I got two. And even if you did, mister, your chances of gettin' it cashed here is one big zero. Who are you?"

"I'm a check gawker."

"Well, I'm a people gawker, and ain't it beautiful how you can never fool an honest face?"

Jim burst out laughing.

"She was a dandy," I told him.

Jim said, "You know what? You oughta move to a small town. You oughta come out here to God's country. You could fill up on good food and write out counter-checks, legal, all the time. You'd be welcome. You'd love it. This place is a jewel!"

Jewell Morning

Greg Michaels

GREG MICHAELS

Journal Entry: Cawker City, 6/6/81

*G*reg Michaels works 150 feet from the world's largest ball of twine. If it were rolled out and stretched east, it would end up in St. Louis, Missouri.

"That's what they claim," said Greg, "but how ya gonna know for sure? It's big, OK, but there's a guy up in Iowa who claims he's got a bigger one. Hell, somebody somewhere has always got something bigger or better. You gotta record, somebody somewhere's gonna beat it."

I agreed. "Do you get tourists coming in here asking about the twine?"

"Not many. Twine's twine."

I saw Greg again in Hunter. It was Friday at Vera's, and things were heating up. Greg was primed. He was on his way to the big dance in Tipton. He pulled up in front of Vera's for a pit stop. He was in his 390 Ford. He revved it up, and the crowd came outside. They wanted to see some action. He revved it up again real loud, and everybody backed off.

On cue, he floored it. The 390 blew smoke, laid rubber, and fishtailed all over Main Street. Greg swerved off the road, then back on it. He shifted into high, laid more rubber, and blew out of town like a rocket. The crowd outside Vera's stood there eating his dust. No one cared about the dust and the noise. This was some good action. Everybody oohed and aahed.

"Did you see that?" somebody said, nudging me.

"He'll be in Tipton before the dust clears!"

The dust settled and, sure enough, the road was empty. There was nothing but the sun on the horizon. Greg was gone. He was in Tipton all right. Who knows, he could have set a record.

As things quieted, one of the dust-eaters hollered, "That's one bad 390!" Another one hollered real loud, "Hot damn, there's gonna be some hell raised in Tipton tooonight!"

And me, I followed up with this: "That was even better than the world's largest ball of twine! But Greg better watch it. It won't be long before somebody somewhere is going to try to beat it, his record time to Tipton."

WE GOT A HERO HERE

Journal Entry: Chapman, Kansas, 8/12/83

I was in Chapman for one reason. What kind of grit did it have? What was its fabric for spawning a hero?

Chapman on this day looked like a morgue. The streets were empty. The wind was the noisiest thing around. The only signs of life I discovered were at the softball field and in the tavern. I went to the tavern first because the air conditioner was on. People are more friendly when they're cool. I sat down next to a small, white-haired man and asked him about Chapman's hero, its native son. Right away, we were overheard.

"Heroes," somebody shouted from the other end of the bar. "We got one here! Astronaut Joe Engle of Chapman, captain of the space shuttle Columbia, Mission 2."

The shouter and the crowd gathered around me. "I've only read about your hero. What's Joe Engle like?"

"Joe's common as salt. You'd never know he's a hero, not by lookin' at him. He looks like one of us. He's all down-home."

"Do you think this town gave him something?"

"Sure," hollered the shouter. "Joe learned to fly on his own, but Chapman taught him to work and play by the rules. Right here, Joe got his values."

The bartender pulled out a newspaper article. We read it aloud.

"Joe Engle, he's a right stuff pilot," the paper said. "He could land a bathtub if one could fly."

"The shuttle," said Engle in the paper, "it's like a used truck."

"Some used truck," I hollered, "a billion dollar one."

"He got that here," said the shouter. "Farm kids learn on trucks."

We read on. "The town of Chapman gave its hero a red-carpet welcome on his return home!" Everybody in the place stood up and cheered. "Boy! You should have been here."

Then I pulled out my journal and read something I had written down from another article. In it, Joe said:

"Looking back down at the world is something that's just hard to describe. I guess you need to back off to really appreciate it. I'm honored to have that opportunity. As you see it from up there, the earth looks limitless."

"That's somethin', ain't it? He's right on the mark. That's our Joe!"

"You know what?" I said when things got quiet. "Joe's done something else. He's done something no other person on this planet has done, not even another astronaut. He's got this one distinction no one can match. Joe Engle was the first person on earth to land a *used* spaceship."

Yes, indeed, used cars, used trucks, Joe flew a used spaceship. The crowd was dumbstruck. All of a sudden, the shouter blurted:

Chapman Softball

"We got a hero and a half now!"

Out at the softball game I sat in the shade, ate peanuts, and looked at the town. I tried to relate to Joe, to outerspace, and to used spaceships. That was tough; then I dwelled on Chapman, Joe, and heroes. That was easy. What appeared to be a frivolous little town this morning now shimmered in the afternoon sun.

Chapman has what it takes, all right. I could feel it. Small towns make plenty of heroes.

POSTSCRIPT: 1/28/86

The Tragedy

In one fiery instant it happened. Challenger exploded. Stunned with disbelief, I, along with every other American, felt the purest pain imaginable.

Joe Engle was here in Kansas when it happened. He was grief stricken. When reached for comment, he had to grope for words. All he could say was that he wanted to get back to Houston and be among his colleagues.

"It had to come someday," said an expert. "We are dealing with speeds and power we've never dealt with before."

I couldn't fathom that remark.

Up to this moment, our success was so commonplace. Joe Engle himself had been up twice. The spectacle of space had become ordinary. I, and maybe all of us, had forgotten the tremendous risk in exploration. Our mastery of mechanization had lulled us to sleep.

The agony of this tragedy leaves with us an indelible reminder. Heroes are pioneers; they pay their dues. Glory and adventure go hand in hand with danger and death. The spirit of discovery always demands sacrifice.

Joe's expression on that awful day said it all. The shuttle crew of the Challenger was the best of us. Their sacrifice will live in our souls forever.

Fort Scott

The License Plate Man, Stanly Mohl

ELLINWOOD
AND THE LICENSE PLATE MAN

Journal Entry: Ellinwood, Kansas, 7/19/81

*I*t was quite a day in Ellinwood. The Old Settlers' Celebration went all the way. They crowned a wheat queen and a wrist wrestling champion. I met the mayor. Today Ellinwood had a beer garden and a tent set up as an open air restaurant. It served chicken and dumplings and homemade pies. There were games, special events, and a parade. I've seen lots of parades, but this was the topper for enthusiasm. The thing went through town twice. That's right, the parade did a double run. "It got going again before we could stop it," said the grand marshal. "I kinda figured, with all the beer being drunk at the garden this morning, that something was gonna happen. But not this, not the parade going through town twice. It's got the schedule all messed up! That bunch that led, they were the ringleaders, that's the end for them. We're gonna put 'em in the rear behind the horses next year. Parades ain't suppose to go twice," he laughed.

Along with the parade and all the enthusiasm, I had one other memorable encounter. Just away from the madding crowd, I met the License Plate Man, Stanly Mohl. His garage is visible from the highway, and every square inch of it is covered with license plates. I stopped early this morning and gave it a thorough inspection. I figured there had to be a character somewhere connected to that garage. Sure enough, no further than the porch next door, tucked up on a step, posing as the quiet, unassuming sort, was my man Stanly. He had two things that set him off. His cap and his glasses. His cap bill was bent up, and his glasses were held tightly around his head with a string of rubber bands.

"Hello, do you know who owns that garage with all those license plates?"

"Yep, it's me," he replied. "They're all mine. I'm the License Plate Man."

"How many's up there?"

"460!"

Oh, boy, I thought to myself. How many people keep track of the exact number of license plates they tack up on the garage?

"That's a lot of license plates."

"I got lots more in my basement and out in the shed. I could cover up the town with 'em. I've got every license plate made in Kansas since 1913. And I know the history of each year, too!"

I stared through Stanly Mohl while he orated about the outstanding differences in license plates. I surmised that anybody who keeps his glasses up with rubber bands and knows license plates frontward and backward is both thrifty and well read. He's a student of tin. And it suits him. He and license plates are a perfect match.

107

"Have you got one from 1949, that's the year I was born?"

"Yep, but only one," he stated. "That's the year they went aluminum. Forty-niners are hard to find."

"Darn," I said, "I was going to buy one."

"There's one on the garage, you want me to get it?"

"No, no, I wouldn't dare put a bare spot on that garage of yours."

"Tell you what," said Stanly. "I'll jump on the first '49er I find. Next time you're this way, look me up."

"Sure thing. I'll come back for a '49er and another license plate lesson."

"One thing before you go, be sure and look at my porch on your way out of town. You'll get a kick out of it."

He grinned while adjusting his rubber bands and glasses.

What would be on the front porch of a thrifty, well-read license plate collector? Exactly. A license plate with numbers that match his street address.

I chuckled to myself and looked back at Stanly over by the garage. He stood there with his arms folded like one of the great collectors of the world. You gotta be pretty good to find a license plate that exactly matches the numbers of your house. Stanly Mohl, I realized, was a professional!

The Bays of LaCygne

Victorian Home, *Washington, Kansas*

Father Hoover

FATHER HOOVER

Journal Entry: Tipton, Kansas, 10/9/81

Father Hoover answered it better than anyone.

After having grown up in a big city, he was assigned and sent off to be the parish priest in the little prairie town of Tipton.

"What's it like for you out here?" I asked him. "Have you adjusted to small-town life?"

With conviction and a big smile he replied, "May the Almighty excuse me for the pun, but this little place is like HEAVEN!"

111

The Tipton Cardinals

EIGHT-MAN FOOTBALL

Journal Entry: Tipton, Kansas, 10/9/81

*I*t's October here in the heartland, and that means it's time for the big event: eight-man football. It's a happening where there aren't many. It's the small-town spectacular that brings people out and pulls them together. In the cafe on game day this is what they say about it.

"It's what we wait for all year long!"

"Eight-man football *is* small-town America!"

"It's our agony and ecstasy."

"Eight-man makes farm boys men!"

I was in Osborne last week when the conditions were perfect. It was the second day after the first big frost, and you could smell autumn in the air. It was just right for football and coming together. It was game day and Osborne was humming. "Let's Go!" posters were tacked up everywhere. The cafe was a constant chatter about the outcome. There was a parade at 4:00 P.M., with banners waving, horns honking, and supporters screaming themselves hoarse. I watched things build to a frenzy. One cheerleader told me she couldn't eat the day of the game. She got so nervous she had to live on chewing gum.

The frenzy was contagious. I went to the game early so I could get on the field close to the action. The sidelines are where football is special. There, you have the noise, the nervousness, and the fathers who pace back and forth. The fathers have their hearts in it beyond compare. Like disciples, they know all the significant details. They have inside information on the blue-chip players, and they are ardent in their support. I wasn't on the sidelines more than five minutes when this big burly fellow with a crewcut and big arms came up to me and said, "That's my boy there, number 66. He's a hitter, keep your eyes on him. He'll rattle some heads around tonight."

At 6:55 it was time. The teams were ready, and the waiting was over. The captains and the band marched out on the field. While the referee flipped the coin, the rest of us stood there shaking, from both the excitement and the cool night air. Then the band struck up the anthem. I got goose bumps, just like the days when I used to play. One father said to me, "It's time for the blood lettin'!" And another one, so nervous he could barely speak, whispered, "This is it!"

Right at kickoff, number 66's father stopped pacing and came up to me. "This is a hot chocolate night, ain't it!"

"It sure is," I replied, "but I'm not leaving this spot to get some, not now!"

"Don't blame ya. I'm not movin' either," he declared. "You ever seen an eight-man game before?"

"You bet," I said.

"They're something else, ain't they?" he bragged. "Eight-man is good basic football, plus action. That's how I like it, nothin' fancy, but plenty of action. You've seen it," he went on, "you know how it goes—the halfback takes a pitch from the quarterback, the end cracks down on the tackle, and if the back gets the corner turned, it's all over. Six points! Touchdown! That's what I love about eight-man," he drooled. "It's a game of breaks. One lucky play and it's all over! Here we go," he hollered, "the kickoff, keep your eye on 66. He'll make something happen. I guarantee it." He went back to pacing and the battle was on.

Today I went to Tipton for another big game. The Cardinals were practicing on the field when I got there. The coach had them going through drills early so that, when the bell rang, they could go straight home, do their chores, and get back in time to be ready for the game and concentrate on winning the "Big One"! "This one's for bragging rights around here," said the coach. "These kids could be hometown heroes come Saturday!"

The coach went on to explain the drama like this. "Tonight this field will be packed with people and surrounded by cars. It's important to win this one. The towns are close and the people overlap. It's a fierce rivalry. It'll be a good one, I promise you that! We got some tough farm kids, but so do they. We're more experienced, but they're hungry. Anything can happen in eight-man. Right now, all I know is this. At seven o'clock, Father Hoover will give the invocation and, then, it's war!"

As the players began to break away for home, I asked them if they were fired up. "Darn right!" they hollered together. Then, with his lip bit in determination, Jimmy Moritz spouted, "We live with this game all year. We gotta win. No," he hollered, "I take that back. We're gonnnnna win!"

It was another perfect night. At the game I stood on the sidelines, got goose bumps, and paced with the fathers. The action was wild and wooly. It had hard hitting and a lot of scoring. There was one lucky play that turned it all around. And the next morning, outside the cafe, I saw Jimmy Moritz and two more Cardinals with their heads up. They were walking tall. They did it. They won the big one!

Country Clothesline

Bill May and His Team

BILL MAY AND HIS HORSEPOWER

Journal Entry: Tipton, 10/12/82

Y ou oughta go see Bill May," they said. "He still plows with a team."
I was apprehensive at first, so I walked slowly up the road and through the gate. When I knocked on the screen door, I said hello with my best smile. "Are you Bill May?"

He suspected I was up to something. Why would anybody want to take pictures of the "old way" of working a field? I told him that history meant something to me. I wanted a feel for the sod-busting days.

Bill May hesitated and sized me up. "That's unusual," he said. "I don't get many visits on account of history. But if that's what you're after, I'd be glad to oblige." Sensing my honesty, he lost his suspicion and warmed up. "Let's go to the barn," he said with a light nod. "I'll show you what I pull the plow with."

The barn had aroma. It smelled of fresh hay and manure. "Meet Molly, Jerry, Gin, and Jack. They're what pull the plow. They're my draft horses and mules. Bona fide flesh and genuine horsepower!"

"What's the difference between them?" I asked.

"Between mules and horses? Temperament," he replied. "Mules are stubborn as hell sometimes. A horse might kick at you. When a mule kicks, they connect! A mule will give you a good day's work, but you gotta be more careful around 'em."

Bill May is a solitary gentleman with a smooth, brown, time-worn face. He has spent long days in the open air. His frame has the same sturdy build as Molly, Jerry, Gin, and Jack. He's the kind of man who looks forward to a good day's work. "Where's the plow?" I asked him. He let the animals out to feed, and we went behind the barn. "This here's what they pull. This is it, a two-bottom gang plow. Ain't it a beaut! It's as old as I am. We kinda go together. We both been at it a long time. I suppose you're wonderin' why me and this old plow are still together.

"It's being your own man that counts. I was born and raised on this place, and I've never owned a tractor. I've kept my principles simple and that ain't nothing to be ashamed of, no sir! Some say I missed out not goin' big time. But I ain't got ulcers, and I ain't in debt either. If you take in account machinery costs and land value, I ain't so sure the big boys are puttin' any more in the bank than me . . . But it's more than that.

"I believe in energy that reproduces itself. The sun, the wind, water, and animals; they do it, too, produce their own energy. We call it horsepower! I love animals. They've been with me all my life. Plowing with a team is in my blood!"

That evening at dusk, we hooked up the team and went to the field. I followed them every step of the way. At a fast pace, I could keep up. We went round and round together. I watched and listened to Bill while he worked his team. He snapped the reins, whistled, and gave out commands. "Get up now. Move in, Gin. Work, Molly, work. Damn it, Jack, stay straight! Get up, Gin. Get up now!"

There was this charge. They had a bond between them. His commands had feeling. He talked to them soothingly. The noises they made were from effort. I felt as if I were walking back in time. We were all in a sweat. Bill was part of the plow. He and the old blade were turning up the ground together. I stayed just behind, in the fresh furrows, because it was soft and I could smell the dark new dirt. On the third time around, Bill stopped the team to rest. They were good and lathered. He patted each of them. "Aren't you tired of following us?" he asked me. "No," I said. "It's really something the way you and the team work together. You've got a bond."

"I love the spirit in these animals. That's real sweat they work up. They don't make the same noise as a diesel tractor. They're quiet. Sure, it's slower, but it's still horsepower. Pure horsepower!

"You know, these animals and me in the field together, well, it's something special," he confessed. "Sometimes it hits me right here in the heart. There's a feeling between me and them: the quiet pull of the reins, the steady canter . . . These animals have feeling. They know love and fear. They respond. And that's what I love about 'em. They're just like people, they hold the element of surprise!"

Bill May, Plowing

ODE TO FLOYD SOWERS

Journal Entry: Mitchell County, 9/12/84

I finally got Floyd Sowers to hold still for once, just long enough to record his likeness.

"You'd better get it right," he clamored. "Why you wanna take my picture? I ain't important. I'm just an ol' Mitchell County farmer."

"You're important to me," I hollered at him.

"Why's that?" he blurted.

"You know why . . . You were born, raised, and stayed in one spot: right here. That's something. And you've got markers, too!"

Floyd Sowers is a tall, lean, leathery man who lives in overalls and believes in work. Prone to silence, he's been a bachelor all his life. He prefers going his own way. But he's a good neighbor, and, if a favor is asked, he's there to do it. I remember the first time I met him, there was a lot of stiffness. Floyd has this stern, preacherlike grimace he carries, and, if you don't know him, he appears standoffish and stubborn at first. But actually it's a front. Floyd Sowers is as bashful as he was on the first day of school.

So why bother Floyd? Because he has a sharp mind, and he remembers things. And if you pester him in the right kind of way, you can get him to recollect and draw on his knowledge.

"What about living out here today?" I asked him. "How do you see farming and rural life?"

"Not good," he stated. "The changes have been too drastic. For a long time the technology we put to use was good. We tamed a hard land with it. But it's gone too far. We're technology dependent. It's made us soft and lazy. It's caused us to lose the values we once had. Today we got too much temptation and not enough spunk!"

"Then the younger generation is spoiled?" I queried.

"I believe you younguns have had it too good. You ain't never felt the hurt we did. My generation struggled along. Nothin' was given to us. Those of us who made it at farmin', made it because we believed in the power of the Almighty, first and foremost. Then we believed in ourselves. That was the guts of it. We got beat, but we never got busted. We never let our spirits break. We knew sacrifice! . . . I just don't know about you younguns!"

"Farmin' will never be the same," he declared. "It's a business now, not a way of life. Farmin' shouldn't be a business. In a business you do things different. You take shortcuts. There ain't no shortcuts in a way of life!"

Floyd makes sense when he talks. And if he's different, it's because he has convictions, and he stands by them. When he says something, it's the bible. He's a stalwart. Someone you can count on. And that's rare in this day and age. I heard a neighbor describe him best.

"Atop them telephone pole legs and rock hard body sits a mind as keen

Floyd Sowers

as a steel trap. Ol' Floyd is a rare commodity. He still seals a promise with a handshake. He never cusses. He's good for an idea. And he falls asleep with the Good Book in his lap. You need a man like that. You need a Floyd Sowers around!"

One night late, on the screened-in porch, Floyd cut loose and expounded on "the markers in his life." Those events that changed him, opened his eyes, and affected him most.

"Change can come like a flurry," he began. "That's the cardinal rule of life.

"My first marker came to me when I was a young boy down on Bacon Creek. It's where I ran onto Indians. Real Indians. I came eyeball to eyeball with 'em. Sioux! They were on their way to the reservation. They scared me something fierce. I froze in my tracks and shook. They just scowled at me. It wasn't 'til later on that I realized they were beaten down and done. But I'll never forget that moment. Real Indians! It was the end of 'em—and the end of the wild frontier.

"Then, I remember when we first got a tractor with rubber tires that had air. Now it may sound silly, but back then it was a big deal: tires with tubes. I remember when it arrived Dad let me drive it to the field. That was comfort, I tell ya. Pure heaven. Like ridin' in a Cadillac. Nothin' ever seemed so nice. The tire and the tube. They brought the onslaught of convenience. They set the stage for modern farmin'.

"Another real marker for me was when Orville and Wilbur Wright got that contraption of theirs off the ground. A flying machine, they had done it. Flown! The word about it spread like wildfire. I listened in disbelief. I just couldn't imagine. How did they do it?, I wondered. Get up in the air and soar like birds?

"But that was nothin'. Along comes Lucky Lindy, and he flies all the way across the Atlantic. I can tell you exactly where I was when that happened. Hoverin' over the radio like a swarm of bees. I, myself, why I've never even seen the ocean. And Lindy, he crossed it sight-unseen! That, I believe, was the most daring feat of our time, bar none!

"An' you know," Floyd chimed, "I actually saw a man set foot on the moon. Right here in my living room. That was my last marker. Did you see that? Boy, that was something. A man on the moon. It showed me that man can go anywhere once he sets his mind to it. You gotta admire our ingenuity, even at the risk of change. That's what's made America. Ingenuity! Havin' these things happen, what a life span I've lived. At this rate, just think about the future. God only knows what the children will be seein'!"

Floyd's recollections amazed me. His markers span an incredible range of change. Think about it. Native Indians to a walk on the moon. What a flurry!

We sat there in silence for a moment, then Floyd said, "What's important about markers is not so much that they happen. No, it's how you react to 'em. How you accept 'em. If you're gonna make it, you gotta have markers. You gotta be ready for change. It can come like a flurry."

That did it. I decided right then to consider my own life's markers. Floyd won't believe it, but I'm starting with him. Like no one else, he put me in touch with the spirit of change.

Doug called today. "L. A.," he said, "ol' Floyd passed away last night. Thought you oughta know. The neighbor who found him said he was there in his rocker, just like always, the Good Book in his lap, and a contented look on his face. She said he looked as if an angel came and got him. If anybody's in heaven, it oughta be him."

"Surely," I replied. "I'm glad he went peaceful. He lived a full life. He'll need no lament. His deeds were his reward . . . You know, Doug, I got a feeling Floyd was ready. He knew his time."

"Yes," Doug whispered. "He was ready. But we weren't. We're gonna miss ol' Floyd more than anybody else!"

Prairie Church

Harvest Buddy, Steve Moritz

HARVEST

Journal Entry: Mitchell County, 7/1/82

*N*othing compared to it. This was the longest day I can ever remember. When the sun finally set, I sighed with relief and hollered out: "My first day of harvest, thank God it's over!"

It was twilight now, and I was waiting for the combine to make its first round of the night. As I waited, I climbed up in the back of the grain truck and laid down on a huge mound of fresh cut wheat. It was time to let my body rest. The first cool breeze of the night blew over me, and I took it easy. I could finally reflect. I mulled over my observations and looked at the notes I had scribbled down during the day, a day that seemed like forever.

NOTE 1

I'm in awe ... Harvest has an energy all its own. It's harder than everyday life, even harder than everyday farm life. It's harder than anything. Sure, I had read about it beforehand. It was supposed to be tough, but nothing read, or said, compared to this. Floyd Sowers said, once, "The only way to know harvest is to be in the middle of it. It'll make you proud you survived!" What Floyd said is sure sinking in today.

There's an urgency about harvest. Livelihoods depend on it. When it's time to cut wheat, nothing else matters. During harvest, farmers change. Their demeanor sways from the usual. They tighten up and get on edge. They step out of character and push hard. They even become possessed to get the work done. Every minute counts. They won't be good ol' boys again until it's all over. Not until the spacious waving fields are nothing but clumps of yellow stubble. Normal people being abnormal, that's harvest. That's what makes it hell-bent.

The sheer pace is confounding. Today was relentless. Everyone and everything were constantly on the move. The combines went ninety to nothing. We drank water out of jugs. We had our meals out of car trunks in the corners of fields. Quitting time, I figured out, is when the dust is so caked on we can no longer open our eyes. At the grain elevator they told me quitting time was when I was so pooped I couldn't take a shower. "No way," I told them. "The dust on me may be as thick as icing, but I'm taking a shower. Even if they have to prop me up, I'm taking a shower."

This day was miserable. Mother Nature was doling out her absolute worst: 110° and not a cloud in the sky, with the wind blistering. It was a scorcher. Facing south felt like standing in front of a blast furnace. The day moved along, not by hours and minutes, but by degrees. This morning was peculiar because it wasn't so bad. It was calm, even cool, early on. But by noon the sun had risen high and every shadow disappeared. The rays beat down on us and a searing mirage engulfed everything. When the wind really picked up,

Spreading Wheat

it was pure hell. There was no refuge anywhere. By late afternoon, the arm I hung out the grain truck window was so sunburned it had water blisters and welts. I wrote down on a grain ticket:

NOTE 2

This is it, a real taste of hell. Out here in the fields everything is in conflict. With the heat, the wind, and us humans in high gear, this isn't harvest, this is a battle. We're at war!

Finally, at 9:00 P.M. it let up. At that moment, when the sun dipped down on the horizon, it cooled. I noticed it immediately. Even the wild wind disappeared. It was uncanny. The sudden tranquility gave me goose bumps. Maybe harvest would be pleasant now.

NOTE 3

I'll never forget this day that seemed like forever. Nor will I forget the reality of July in these wide open spaces. And with it, the absolute meanings of morning, noon, and night.

As the stars came out and the elements continued to alter, I felt an unusual kind of melancholy. The kind that only comes after a long, all-out day. The battle was almost over. The cool breeze that blew over me now had a rejuvenating freshness. The warm wheat I was lying on tingled my back. I breathed easy and gazed up at the stars. My mind wandered to something I had studied but never taken to heart—not until now. It was about the things I was finally in the middle of: man, wheat, and harvest.

Thousands of years ago, wheat was nothing more than a grass growing wild in the Fertile Crescent.

But then man came along, discovered it, tendered it, and made it into bread. He planted it, harvested it, and tamed the wild grass called wheat. He built his life around it. And, because of it, he ceased to roam.

Thus the nomad became the agrarian. This happy conjunction caused something momentous. At that moment, thousands of years ago, when man met wheat, civilization began!

Civilization! What a feeling! Lying here in the back of a grain truck, under a blanket of stars on a hot harvest night, staring off at the combine on the horizon, I couldn't help but feel the connection between man, wheat, and thousands of years of harvest. We are a far cry from the nomad and the wild grass of the Fertile Crescent. Since man met wheat, we've come a long way together.

Oh, Civilization, finally I can vouch for it.

Harvest

Threshing Queen, Laura Rudder

THRESHING QUEEN

Journal Entry: Bird City, Kansas, 7/30/83

I deserve this," declared Laura Rudder. "We womenfolk are worthy of more recognition. We were a big part of pioneering.

"I fed many a threshing crew in my younger days. Harvest time for us women was just as hard as you could imagine.

"Nowadays they talk how tough it was in the fields. But let me tell you, it was no picnic in the kitchen either. We got up long before the men to get out breakfast. As soon as we fed them and the dishes were done, we started right in on dinner. Then we baked pies and bread for the next day. Then we got started in on supper. It was hot and just as hard as man's work. We kept our men going. If you were a woman and you worked harvest, you'd agree, they couldn't have made it without us. As far as I'm concerned, *all* us pioneering women deserve to be queens!"

Summer Storm

GOD BLESS AMERICA
AND THE SINGLE EAGLE SALUTE

Journal Entry: Bogue, Kansas, 7/24/81

*H*ere it was, early on a July morning and my journal already had sweat on it. I was after some eggs and coffee before the sun got high enough to burn my appetite. On my way to the cafe, I came across a cool slab of concrete inviting enough for a pause. I was sitting in the shade of "God Bless America," listening to the cafe door creak open and bang shut when a truckload of hell-raisers pulled up and poured out onto the curb. They were smashed. It was 8:00 A.M. Tuesday.

"Who are you?" they asked.

"A tourist," I replied.

"The hell you are. That ain't no Brownie camera you got there."

"OK," I said, "I'm documenting life on the Great Plains."

"In Bogue?"

"Everywhere."

"Document us," said Sonny Newell, the ringleader.

"OK. Why are you smashed?"

"It's a special occasion."

"Tuesday, 8:00 A.M.?"

"Yep," said Sonny, "we been up all night drillin' for oil. We're roughnecks on the graveyard shift. When we finish one, we celebrate."

"Did you strike it rich?"

"We don't know. The geologist tests for oil. We just drill 'em. We don't give a damn about the outcome. What we celebrate is gettin' done!"

"Hey, you gonna document us?"

"I sure am."

"When?"

"Right now."

"Then where you want us?"

"Right where I was. Right under the sign."

"What you gonna call us?"

"Let's see. How's this—God Bless America and the Smashed Rough-necks. Look patriotic now. Smile and say God Bless America."

"OK, boys," said Sonny, "let's be real patriotic. Let's say God Bless America and let's give him the single eagle salute!"

God Bless America

VERA AND WILLIE

Journal Entry: Hunter, After Many Visits

*W*hat a pair, Vera and Willie!

Vera Lewis is *the* main attraction in Hunter. She runs the pool hall and performs. She's renowned. I've been all the way to Russia and back, and I haven't seen the likes of her anywhere. She has no bashful bones in her body. She keeps the pool hall lively at all times with her yodeling, dancing, and the singing of her favorite song, "On the Wings of a Snow White Dove." Since I first started coming to Hunter, she has probably yodeled, danced, and sung "On the Wings of a Dove" 2 million times. She performs at the drop of a hat. If you want to get Vera going, all you have to do is wink and say, "Vera, do 'On the Wings.' " Without hesitation, she will stop whatever she's doing and bellow it right out, country style, with all her feeling.

It's an experience, Vera's performing. "On the Wings" is her trademark, and it affects everybody who comes to the pool hall. It especially affects the regulars. They've nearly OD'd on it. They always holler out when Vera stops and sings. "Who did it? Who turned her on? Damn it, here we go again!"

You see, when Vera sings, business stops. Service in the pool hall comes to a screeching halt. During "On the Wings," the beer and soda she's carrying gets hot. And that's what gets the regulars hollering: hot beer and soda. "She's like a juke box," said one of them, "only you can't turn *her* off. You can't pull the plug on Vera, not during 'On the Wings of a Dove!' "

Vera lives with enthusiasm. I've taken friends to Hunter, and they still shake their heads about seeing and being at Vera's. In good form, she's just short of a spectacle. Wound up, she's worth the price of admission. You should see her when we coax her into a grand finale. She'll stand up on the counter for added effect. "I've been to a circus that wasn't as good as Vera's," said one out-of-towner.

Knowing Vera has been a plus. She has a rosy disposition. She's good-natured to the core. She puts up with a lot of commotion in the pool hall business, and it never gets her down. That's her strong point, she takes everything in stride. In fact, I've never even seen her frown—except once. It concerned Willie.

Willie Waddle is one of the strong points of American variety. He beats to a different drum. Compact, spry, and devilish, Willie likes to cause trouble. His favorite thing is to "fuzz folks up." He's famous for it. What Willie calls "fuzzin'" is another term for creating general havoc on the public. I was at Vera's when the "Big Quake" occurred, and Willie was the first accused of causing it. That directly led to a confrontation with Vera. That ended up in what everybody around Hunter calls "The Great Chase"!

The Big Quake incident was the only time I ever saw Vera get beet red with anger, and who else but Willie would be at the bottom of it? I call Willie

Willie and Vera, "What's Up?"

Willie and Vera, "Making Up"

Willie, "Back in Good"

"the ornery little elf." The Big Quake incident went like this.

It was Saturday night, and there was a good crowd gathered at Vera's. As usual, all of a sudden, Willie popped in primed for "fuzzin'." Right away, the crowd got on Willie before he could get on them. The night before, somebody had rammed into the side of the pool hall with a vehicle. The second Willie came storming through the pool hall door, it started. Willie was the one who had caused the "Quake." Yep, it was his Dodge, and he in it that rammed into the side of Vera's at 15 mph, knocking the beef jerky and pickled eggs off the shelf, sending cigarettes, candy, and anything not attached to the bar flying. Willie, of course, denied it.

It's elementary, no one ever admits to things in Vera's. They just pass the blame around. The last accused or the one not present is usually the culprit for the last bit of trouble caused. But this time it was different. It was all Willie on the "Quake." The crowd hammered away at him.

"Willie, you're the one," they hollered. "You rammed Vera's. You caused the 'Quake.' You knocked everything off the wall. Where were you last night? There's paint on your bumper. Come on, Willie, admit it, you did it!"

Willie just shook his head.

Meanwhile, all the accusations against Willie got Vera stirred up. Repairing the counter was still fresh in her mind. So, finally, Vera lost that smile of hers and went up to Willie and put it to him point blank. "Willie, did you ram the wall?"

There was a long silence, and Willie said nothing. He just smiled. Well, that was it. We all knew what that meant: yes, yes, and yes! Vera got beside herself. She lost all composure. She picked up a pool stick and chased Willie out the door and right down Main Street. It's a good thing Willie is quick. You should have seen the two of them. Vera in flight and Willie in fright. There are those who still claim that was "The Great Chase."

It took Vera a while to get over the Big Quake incident. Willie was banned from the pool hall for a while. He had to take his orneriness to the street. He hung out on the corner and fuzzed up passersby. Vera was tough on him this once. "You see," she said, "every once in a while, there's a price for fuzzin' folks up, and Willie knows it!"

But, in all fairness to Willie, at times you've got to look past his outright orneriness. He's got another side. There is a true sense about him. He loves Hunter and everybody in it. The place is his number-one stomping grounds and home sweet home. He even has a dream about Hunter. Someday, when his time comes, he'd like to die right on the main street of Hunter. Just like Ol' Man Helvy did. Willie thinks it's something how Helvy got his wish. Ol' Helvy told Willie a long time ago he wanted to go to heaven in Hunter.

"And, by golly, he did," said Willie. "Ol' Helvy died right here on the main street of Hunter. He was doin' 5 mph in his truck. About even with the cafe, he just slumped over and died. Spike Dieter was with him, and he got the truck stopped but, for Ol' Helvy, it was too late. He was already on his way up. It shook Spike, but it was OK 'cause Helvy got his wish. He went up to heaven in Hunter!

"Now, I mean," grinned Willie, "ain't that a way to go! That's my wish. I want to be lucky, just like Ol' Man Helvy. When I go, I want it to be right here on the main street of Hunter. It'd be great, I reckon, if I went up at Vera's or about even with the cafe."

Willie, "On Main Street"

Vera, "In Good Form"

VERA'S:
ONCE UPON A HAPPY HOUR

Journal Entry: Hunter, Kansas, 5/30/85

I hadn't been to Hunter for a while so, when I crossed those familiar tracks, I took a quick right and went straight to the Co-op station. There I paid my respects and declared, "There'll be Happy Hour at Vera's today. I'm buying the first round!" Then I went to Mary and Doug's.

When Doug and I came back to town at noon, word had spread like wildfire. Walking down Main Street, everybody we saw yelled, "Hot dog, today there's Happy Hour." Red Jensen's boy saw us and yelled from clear down by the meat locker, "Hey, L.A., I hear there's Happy Hour, and you're buying!" "Oh, hell," Doug sighed. "What have you gone and done?" "Excitement," I declared, "I'm ready for some excitement." "You're going to

Vera and Gus, "Primed"

139

Vera and Gus, "Cuttin' a Rug" part 1

get it," Doug laughed. "It ain't even one o'clock, and you've already got the whole town stirred up!"

Five o'clock came quick. Vera was ready, and the place was packed. It just takes one stranger or half an excuse for things to get riled up in Hunter. It takes even less than that for Vera's eyes to twinkle. They were sparkling.

Right away she gave me a big hug and kiss. "What'll ya have, L.A.?"

"Give everybody a round, Vera, and give me a song and a dance."

"OK," she hollered while plunking in the cooler for beer and soda. She grabbed an armload and yodeled. Larry Cheney jammed the jukebox full of quarters and punched "On the Wings of a Dove." Melvin Keller reached behind it and turned it up full blast. Vera started singing, and it was official: Happy Hour was on.

Next, Gus came in. He ordered two Colorado Kool-Aids and a dance. "With who?" Vera asked. "With you!" he demanded. "Will ya mind the cooler?" Vera asked me. "Sure," I said. "Let's go," said Gus.

"Wait a minute," hollered Bobby Wiles. "Vera, go put on one of them T-shirts that look like you." "I can't," said Vera. "I only got smalls." "That's OK," said Bobby, "squeeze into one. You can do it. It's Happy Hour, L.A.'s in town, and it's good advertisement." "OK," she giggled and disappeared. She came back to a round of applause. She did it. Somehow she squirmed into a small. "Now we're cookin'. Back off," hollered Bobby, "Vera and Gus are cuttin' a rug!"

Somebody put on the foot stompin' music, Gus grabbed Vera, and the two of them went to town. While passing out refreshments, I took it all in. Happy Hour in Hunter. What a spectacle! Vera was primed and Gus was smashed. The jukebox blared and the floor shook. Gus was handling Vera like a bobcat. He twirled, flipped, and stepped all over her. Vera followed, like the other bull in a china closet.

There was other commotion. Gronewaller and Willie were playing one-handed catch with the pool balls. Ronnie Heller was smashing beer cans and shooting hook shots at the trash barrel. The cans were flying everywhere. Terry Heller was hee-hawin' and pounding on the bar. Max Keller was calling the dance. "Ladies and Gentlemen, here we have in the fair city of Hunter, Gus, better known as Fred Astaire, and Vera, the Wild Bohemian Woman!" I laughed and was thankful. The peace and quiet people were long gone.

Then Sas walked in. He was stopping in for the usual: one cool and quiet one. Inside the door he surveyed the madness and laid into me. "What are you doin' behind the bar? Did you start this? This place is a zoo. Give me my cold one for the road. I sure ain't stayin' here. Where's Red? You ran him off, didn't ya? You sure know how to stir up a man's constitution." Sas left, and I looked at Doug. He grinned, "He'll get over it—about next week!"

Happy Hour accelerated. General havoc continued 'til midnight. When Doug and I slipped out, Vera was soppin' wet but still going strong. Gus was gone, but there were others to take his place. The floor was still shaking. Doug said to me just out the door, "You made this a night to remember." "It wasn't just me," I told him, "never underestimate the power of Happy Hour, especially at Vera's."

The next day I took two aspirins and went over to Ham and Mary Keller's. Mary wanted the low-down since she and some of the wives don't go into Vera's very often.

"Did Vera yodel?" she asked.

"Of course."

"Did she dance?"

"Better than ever."

"Did she sing 'On the Wings?'"

"Fifty times."

"Did she get on the counter?"

"Yep, Bobby Wiles, Cheney, Doug, and I helped her up there."

"You know," said Mary. "We got a rare one in Vera. One time I saw her do the jig at the post office in front of the Methodist minister."

"This was better than that," I explained to her. "This was a happening. Vera and Gus were in rare form and everybody followed suit."

"I can imagine," said Mary. "There's only one Vera's. And that's all we need!"

Vera and Gus, "Cuttin' a Rug" part 2

Delmer Gier

WHEN SHE BLOWS, SHE BLOWS

Journal Entry: On The Great Plains, All The Time

*A*in't no two ways about it," claimed a prairie farmer. "If you live out here, you live with the wind.

"Prevailing is the word they use, but that's too nice. Blow, beat, and bang are better. Best is perennial. All the time, we get the wind. Out here there ain't nothin' to stop it. When she blows, she blows!

"Our wind can flat bend ya back, blow ya over, or stop ya straight. It can make a windsock so straight you'd think it was carved out of somethin'. I've seen it blow chickens plumb off the ground. We got trees in these parts that, due to the damned wind, lean permanent. That ain't no joke. You ever try to walk in a 50 mile-an-hour gust? It'll stop you straight. Some folks think that's blarney, but it ain't, not out here.

"To us in these parts, it's unusual when she don't blow. That's when we get nervous. When it's dead calm, it's time to look around."

The Wind, *Kingman County*

The Wind, *Goessel, Kansas*

POOL HALL TALK

Journal Entry: Small Town Pool Halls, Often

On the backroads all over the Great Plains there's no place like the pool hall. It's the one vital piece of property in a prairie town. Through it flows the gossip and the stories that give a town its color.

I use the pool hall like a library. It's where I get my raw material. It's where I learn about the characters who give a place its grit. I'm never in the pool hall very long before I hear a story. Here are a few I have highlighted in my journal.

CLOSER TO ALASKA

It was 103° one Saturday in Kanopolis. I hit the pool hall in late afternoon, parched. I wiped my brow, got something cold to sip on, and looked around at the misery.

Pool halls are testy when the temperature gets over 100°. I had no sooner wet my whistle when somebody banged through the door and hollered loud enough for everyone in the whole place to hear, "Golly, it's cold here. I just came from Brookville, and I swear there it's 106. Go to Brookville, you can feel the difference. Don't know why," he proclaimed, "but there's a difference between 103 and 106. It's colder here, sure enough!" There was a long pause and some wide-eyed stares.

Then Dave Stroede stood up and said, "Hell, it ought to be colder here. We're 30 miles closer to Alaska."

440 COOL

No one knew the exact temperature, but it was hot enough in Sun City that you couldn't ignore it. I was at Hathaway's Place with Tom Smith. Tom, Buster, and I were drinking tomato reds and discussing perseverance. Tom and Buster recollected how different it was growing up. Tom remembered the first type of air conditioning known.

"When I was a kid there was only one kind of air conditioning. We called it 440 Cool. It wasn't like turning on a machine. No sir. You got 440 Cool by getting out of the house and into the car. You got in the car, rolled down all four windows, and took off. You got the car up to 40 and hoped like hell the wind cooled you off. That was 440 Cool. It and ice was all we had."

Cotton Hay's Place

"And ice didn't help much," said Buster. Tom looked out at the heat and said, "Damn, Buster, today I wonder how we ever survived."

BEING NEIGHBORLY

In this pool hall one day I ended up at the bar in between two farmers who live just down the road from each other. Because they were neighbors and because I was interested in neighborliness, they defined it for me in their own particular way. Neighborliness is relative, according to them.

"We're close," said one. "We're connected," said the other. "There's a farm between us, but we're still connected."

"How's that?" I asked.

"Well," said one, "the wind blows his dirt on my place in the summer, and it blows my dirt on his place in the winter. That makes us what you call 'down-to-earth neighbors,' don't it? We exchange each other's dirt."

"That leads to the good part," they both declared. "We got to come here to the pool hall to talk about it, complain, and wash it all down."

HEAD FOR COVER

One day at the Play-Mor in Ellsworth, these old-timers were huddled around a card table talking and playing checkers. I overheard one of them say, "Remember the twelve-bottom gang plow? Remember how we thought it was huge? Hell, it ain't nothin' compared to today. I was out on the highway this morning, and I seen an ol' boy pullin' a disk with a Versatile. The two of 'em were bigger than a fillin' station. The ol' boy was takin' a swath wide as the highway. I said to myself, Chrissakes, if they keep makin' machinery bigger, someday we're gonna have to head for cover. Implements are startin' to look like shoppin' centers, and I'm startin' to feel like a quail."

TORNADO WARNING

It was storming outside, and it got quiet when somebody said tornado. It always gets quiet when pool hall talk turns to tornadoes.

"We live with a lot of false alarms," one tornado expert declared. "But, if you ever catch a glimpse of one, or ya stand in the middle of that peculiar calm, or if ya ever been blown away, that's it, you're in the club. You become a chicken-little. I've been in that calm. I'm one.

Sun City, Kansas

"Nowadays when I see a cloud, or I hear a warnin', I go for cover. It just takes one close call to humble ya. Tornado warnin's in these parts is somethin' all us chicken-littles take serious. By the way, what's it doin' outside? Let's go check that sky!"

A HAIL STORM STORY

"You wanna hear a good hail storm story?" this character asked me.
"Sure," I said, "if it's a true one."
"You bet it is! Jerry, this buddy of mine, was out in a field one day when the wind changed, the temperature dropped, and a big black cloud brought in some nasty weather. It started to hail. When the hail stones got bigger than mothballs, he figured he'd better head for shelter. He was about to get goin' when they got bigger yet, somewhere between golfball-size and baseball-size, accordin' to him.

"When they got that big, he decided to jump out of the truck and grab himself a souvenir. He was gonna brag on what he found. He figured, ain't nobody gonna believe the size of these babies. Well, he hopped out like an idiot, and a big un' conked him on the head. Smacked him good. He picked it up, got back in the truck, saw stars, and conked out. He went out cold for a while.

"When he came to, he discovered he was bleeding from the gash where he got hit, so he drove into town and got his head sewed up at the hospital. Meanwhile, the souvenir that gave him the conk had been meltin'. By the time he got it home to the freezer, it was back down to golfball-size.

"When he comes in the pool hall these days, we sure give him the business. He got a souvenir all right, but it wasn't hail. It was stitches. Golfball-sized hail don't turn heads around here. Stitches do. Yep, he lost his braggin' rights on his souvenir hail, and we tell him, too. Then we ask him to show us his head. That's how we know he wasn't exaggeratin', not one bit!"

"It's a Whopper," Vera's

Logan Boys: Harold Dye, Wilson Lafferty, Jake Noel, Ted Harmon

GOD'S COUNTRY

On a rather warm day at the pool hall in Scott City an elderly couple came in for some soda and the cool air. They sat down right next to me because they wanted to be friendly to a stranger. In the course of our conversation they bragged and reassured me that, "Yes, this part of the world was God's country, but not just now. Come back and see us when it's cooler. It'll seem more like God's country then!"

"When will that be?" I asked them. "When should I come back?"

"Let's see," they pondered, "after summer and before winter, or after winter and before summer."

LOGAN

The Logan pool hall used to be Frank Noel's Dry Goods. "It had everything," said Jake Noel. "Come with me, I'll show ya." Jake and I went downstairs to the musty old basement. Jake rummaged through boxes and crates and found old receipts from the dry goods days.

"Look here," he said, "1920: soap 9¢, Borax 14¢, eggs 44¢. Here's 1921: fly paper 10¢, bacon 38¢, coffee 45¢ a pound. 1923: Bull Durham 5¢, shoes $3.80, night shirts $1.85. I told ya Frank had everything."

We went back upstairs and Jake and his buddies reminisced, but not about dry goods. Harry Sammons came in and sat down at the old oak bar. I ended up over by him. Harry overheard Jake and his buddies so he reminisced, too.

"You've heard of the Dirty Thirties, haven't ya?"

"Many times," I said. "People worked for a dollar a day."

"It was worse than that. It wasn't the money, it was the dirt. You can't imagine the dust. It'd be clear, then all of a sudden you would see a black wall. And if you're wonderin' what was behind it, it was dirt! Miles and miles of dirt. Three or four days of it.

"You ever seen the pictures some people got? You could be in the front seat of your car and not see the hood. That's how bad it was. It'd get pitch black. Everything everywhere had a fine layer of dust. We looked chocolate, but we sure didn't taste it. There were some folks who actually died of dust pneumonia. Terrible.

"What topped that," declared Harry, "we were still in the grips of Prohibition. Those of us who lived it were broke, dirty, and dry! One of the worst periods in our history. No more needs to be said about it. Just be thankful, you young kids are lucky. Broke, dirty, and dry, I wouldn't wish on anyone!"

WIDE OPEN

At Cotton Hay's place in Oakley you can see the cash register open all the time. "Is it stuck?" I asked him. "Nope," he said. "It's old, but it ain't stuck."

"Then why don't you shut it or put your money under the counter where it's safe?"

"No need for that, it's against my principles. I know ever'body who comes through that door, and it ain't money they're after. Me, the cash register, and this part of the world are all the same—wide open!"

Harry Sammons

Pancake Gal

THE PANCAKE GALS

Journal Entry: Liberal, Kansas, 2/23/82

The pancake race at Liberal is international. Kansas runs against England, and Liberal runs against Olney. It got started years ago with a challenge. On Shrove Tuesday, the women of Liberal and Olney dash through the streets of their towns with skillets and pancakes, hoping to beat the clock and set a record time. Both distances are the same. And each year, moments after the race, the towns hook up by long distance and compare times. The officials then declare the winner: woman, town, and country!

Hearing so much about it, I went to get caught up in the excitement and look at the gals. I wanted to photograph someone pretty. Right away I felt the frenzy. People showed up from everywhere. The media was out in full force. And, as one fellow put it, "Anybody's liable to end up on TV at the pancake race." There was even a dignitary from England.

I got there early enough to watch the gals warm up, and even that's different. There's a serious attitude about them. They've all trained hard. Each one wanted to win.

Nowadays things are streamlined. They run with lightweight skillets. They told me the Teflon-coated ones are the best. The official pancakes are even different. They feel like lightweight rubber. I wouldn't eat one on a bet.

Just before the gun went off, I positioned myself near the finish line in the middle of the crowd. I ended up next to an owl-eyed official who was proud to give me every fact and detail he thought I needed to know.

"It's required that each runner flip the pancake during the race. And some of it's gotta be in the pan when they cross the line. The rest is just speed. Good runners win this thing, not good flippers!"

"Why you here?" he asked me. "You from some newspaper?"

"No, I'm looking to photograph one of the gals."

"Stick with me, I'll get ya a picture of the winner."

"No," I said, "she doesn't have to be the winner. I just want a picture of a wholesome gal, the All-American Type."

"I got ya. You just point her out, and I'll go get her. Here they come," he hollered.

I focused on them coming down the stretch. They crossed the line exhausted and looked spent. The owl-eyed official looked at me. "Which one?"

"I don't know yet," I hollered, "they look too tired." Then we got lost in the crowd. Darn, I thought to myself. . . .

Then I felt a tug. There he was, the owl-eyed official, nudging me with a pancake gal on his arm. "How's this one?" She blushed. I winked and said, "Perfect." I took her picture, and he went for another, just in case. They all looked wholesome to him.

He came back to me and said, "Boy, this is fun, fetchin' pretty women! You know what I like about our gals in these parts? They're not only wholesome, they're the homespun, no-nonsense type. They look good with their makeup off. I like that. You know what you're gettin'. Out here, ever' man needs a woman like that! Yessir, our women out here are homespun, no-nonsense gals. I'd put 'em up against women anywhere!"

He was about to fetch another one when somebody climbed up on the platform and tapped on the microphone. "I have the times," he announced. "By two-tenths of a second, this year's winner is from . . . LIBERAL!"

Bedlam broke out. The owl-eyed official and the rest of the pancake gals disappeared into the pandemonium. Darn, I'd have to look for something pretty somewhere else.

Harvest Queen, Angela Leach

Amish Mennonite Girls, *Partridge, Kansas*

Loren and John

Albert Greiner

ALBERT GREINER AND OLD RING

Journal Entry: Haviland, Kansas, 6/30/83

*A*lbert Greiner used to have a dog. Old Ring was his name. He was a sheep dog and, according to Albert, "as good as they come!" Old Ring could round 'em, break 'em out, and bring 'em back better than any dog he'd ever seen. "He ran circles around sheep," said Albert. "And I was damn glad to own him!"

Whenever it was time to move the sheep to the pasture south of the highway, Old Ring was "something else," said Albert. "His ears would perk up and he'd bounce. He could smell the danger and looked forward to it. Along the highway he worked them sheep like a champion. In all Ring's years we never lost a single sheep on that highway!"

Old Ring was special all right, even down to his daily routine. He went everywhere that Albert went. And, when it came to riding along in the truck, that was special, too. Old Ring didn't ride in the back of the truck, like most dogs. No, he rode on top of the truck! "Yes, sir," said Albert, "he rode everywhere I went, smack-dab on the top of the cab! Damndest thing you ever saw," said Albert. "A dog on top of a truck, content as can be!

"And here's the good part," goes Albert. "One day I decided to get rid of that truck, trade it in—the time had come. That truck had seen better days. So I went and bought a brand spankin' new one with air conditioning and the works. Couldn't wait to show it to Old Ring. It had a nice cab, too. Well, I woke up that next morning and Old Ring was gone. It scared hell outta me. It wasn't like him to leave home without me. So I got in my new truck and went looking for him.

"Old Ring wasn't down on the highway. So I headed back to town to talk with the kids. I was driving right down Main Street when I spotted him. Guess where Old Ring was—the used car lot, row one, on the top of the cab of that old truck of mine! I cracked up! I stopped, got out of that brand spankin' new truck, went over to him, and said, 'Ring, you come down now!' He looked at me with that tail of his thumpin' on the top of that cab—and he didn't budge an inch.

"Well, you can probably guess the rest of the story. I went home, got the checkbook, and went back and rebought my old truck, with Ring on it—and then drove it, with him on it, 'til the day he died!"

Weathered Barn, *Allen County*

Doug and Lee with Skins

The Draw

THE HUNT

Journal Entry: Mitchell County, Kansas, 12/4/83

There are those experiences that jolt you!

On this grisly winter morning, marked by a gray sky and a stiff wind, we took off to the fields looking for a buck deer with a big rack. Doug had the license. Max was along as lookout. And I was after some "unvarnished truth," be it good or bad.

We squeezed into the cab of Doug's pickup with guns, ammo, and provisions. High-spirited and poised, we were ready for anything that moved. The heater roared as we meandered through open country keeping an eye out. We ate cookies, drank coffee, and told stories most of the morning. The guns were in the rack behind us, unloaded and at ease. My feelings were mixed. I wanted to know about hunters, yet I was not excited about seeing a kill. I felt queasiness, but it was covered by our camaraderie and the comfort of the cab. So far, we were having fun with the stories and just when I thought we would do this all day, it happened. Max saw something.

He picked up the field glasses and beamed in on a gray dot along the rim of a bluff. The dot was a deer. The meandering was over. The hunt was on. Silence fell, Doug and Max tensed up, and we were off like warriors. The queasiness I felt went right to my stomach.

To me, deer are graceful and innocent creatures, and I don't own a gun. But there is another side to this story. Deer are wild game, and they eat crops and trample fields. The other men in the cab knew this version. They told me that the deer population was too thick this year. It was time to thin them some. "Besides," said Doug, "we're hunters. This license proves it!"

"Does their innocence affect you?" I asked.

"No way," said Max as he jammed the chamber full of bullets. "When you're born out here, hunting is part of growing up. You don't feel sorry for wild animals. If we don't get 'em, Mother Nature will!"

It was "all out" now. We pressed hard, ripping across the pasture. "He went over the ridge," hollered Max. "Get on it!"

"Did we lose him?" asked Doug. "Damn!" they both groaned. I calmed inside. We tore through a meadow and up to the top of a ridge. Max got a bead on him again. "He's there" he hollered, "in that milo field!" Doug put it in high gear. Max kept the glasses pressed to his face. My stomach churned. "Circle from the south," said Max. "I think he's stopped. I think he's holdin' tight in that patch of milo. Let's go on foot."

Doug put on the brakes, we threw open the doors, grabbed the glasses, guns, and ammo, and lit out. We ran through a draw, then crept up to the milo like Indians. Max whispered, "He's layin' low all right. He ain't movin'. He's foxin' us. This ain't gonna be easy."

"Let's go up on that ridge," Doug whispered back. "We'll lose him from here. This milo's too tall." Max nodded yes.

One at a time, we dashed to the ridge, knelt down, and waited. Time crawled. I watched Doug. He cradled the rifle in his lap. I could see his heartbeat in his neck. Max kept frozen with the glasses glued on the milo. I felt butterflies. The anticipation was excruciating.

Finally, something happened—the milo moved. "I see him," whispered Max. He handed me the glasses. "Look there," he pointed. I surveyed the milo and spotted him, a strong, young buck. His innocence was in my throat.

Max took the glasses back. "Is he in range?" Doug asked.

"Not yet. Wait 'til he comes out of that milo." Doug had sweat dripping off his brow. I grimaced. Up on that ridge, you could have cut the adrenalin with a knife. Doug and I watched Max. We waited for his lips to move. Finally they did. He hollered, "Now, Doug, get him!"

Doug stood up, beaded in, and aimed. I closed my eyes and cringed. It was the moment of truth. A big-sounding crackle rang out and deafened my eardrums. I opened my eyes and jumped up. The buck took off. He was running full speed through the field. I blinked. He never broke stride. I couldn't believe it. Doug must have missed him. We pursued. My mouth was like cotton. These were men I admired, but on this hunt I hoped they would lose. My heart was with the buck. "Get going!" I cheered him under my breath.

Moments later we got to a clearing near the creek bottom. Doug and Max examined the ground. They found spots of blood. My heart sank. The shot had rung true. We followed the trail.

Across the creek it was the end. The hunt was over. The young buck was dead. The carcass lay quiet in the grass, still warm and lathered. In the glazed-over gray eyes, I saw no pain, but I felt real pity. The buck had been gallant in flight. We stood there letting the adrenalin drain, and no one said a word.

Max and Doug then went about field dressing the buck with efficiency and respect. The warm innards they pulled out lay in a colorful heap on the ground. I stared at them. My eyes fixed on the crimson heart. Steam rose up from it. The hunt, every second of it, flashed back through my mind. The heart that pounded perpetually just moments ago would never beat again.

They hung the buck in a tree to let the last of the blood drain, and we talked about it. They were triumphant hunters, and I got my "unvarnished truth."

Deep down, it was a bitter ending for me. All I could feel in that creek bottom was the desolation and emptiness that death leaves. The steaming heart will forever remain the grim reminder that life and death are commonplace in the wild. There are no compromises between hunters and the hunted, only winners and losers. It is not pretty, but it is real. And someday we must all see it.

The Buck

The Unvarnished Truth

The Kaw

BABE'S HAVEN

Journal Entry: Haysville, Kansas, 11/19/82

*B*abe Webb's place is a haven for animals who are homeless. They flock in, migrate, and just show up at Babe's.

"People drop 'em off, and sometimes I go rescue 'em," she said. "It's known. This place is a sanctuary. Who could turn their back on a poor animal?"

"The ones that flock in, how do they know to get here?" I asked her.

"It's like they got feelers," she said. "Some kind of radar. Animals are smart. They can sense a home."

Babe took me around and showed off her haven. She had makeshift shelters all over the place. In nooks and crannies were geese, guineas, goats, turkeys, pigs, and chickens. Some were lame. All had been neglected. But, now at Babe's, they were out of harm's way.

It was different here all right. I noticed it when the dogs didn't bark, when the cats and chickens walked between my legs, and when I saw every bird in the county roosting in the trees.

"Babe, there's something about this place," I told her. "I can feel it."

"Yes," she replied, "there is something about this place, and these animals know it. In these parts, it's the safest place in the world."

Babe Webb

JOHN GRIEB'S HEART OF AMERICA

Journal Entry: Lebanon, Kansas, 9/14/81

Some say there is special energy at the center of things. For that reason, I stopped to read the sign on the highway that said "Geographic Center of the United States just ahead." By way of a slight detour, I could stand on the spot that is considered the very heart of America. Maybe there would be some special energy there? Perhaps I would get a jolt of some kind, a feel for the very soul of America. Curiosity had me. The detour was on.

Ten minutes later I found it: a roadside park with a stone marker and a bronze plaque. My first impression was ordinary. "This place is perfect to pull over and sleep." It was the end of a long day so I got comfortable and wound down. I relaxed and waited for the jolt, but nothing happened. I waited 'til it got dark, but still nothing. No special energy, just a plaque and a marker in a park. The only stir again came from curiosity. Who used to own this spot? Whose place was the heart of America?

I went to the first farmhouse I could find and learned that it was John Grieb who once owned the land where the marker sits and that he lived just down the road a ways. I went down the road a ways, and, as chance would have it, I went to the wrong place, but also, as chance would have it, he was there, visiting the neighbors. I knocked, the neighbor told me to wait on the porch, and he went and got John.

"John Grieb, I'm interested in your spot that's now the heart of America. Can you tell me about it?"

"What?" he hollered. "Speak up!"

"Did you own the heart of America once?"

"Yeah, but yell at me. I'm hard a hearin'!"

"Can I take a picture of you tomorrow by the marker and plaque?"

"Why you wanna take my picture?" he shouted with a leery look.

"Nostalgia!" I shouted back.

"Ain't nobody done that before!" he bellowed.

"They should have," I bellowed back.

John Grieb, at the Heart of America

Our repartee intensified. We screamed on and roused up the barnyard. Dogs got to barking. Cats ran for cover. The lights came on across the road. "We woke up the neighbors," he screamed, louder than ever, and more lights came on. I stepped back and realized this was the jolt. We were having a hollering match. My tonsils hurt. "OK," he finally yelled, "I'll meet you in the morning."

Bright and early, there he was, thumbing through the visitors' book by the marker on the spot. He looked bashful, but proud. That all-important book was something he made possible. It caused him to be nostalgic.

"It was 1940 when I learned that my land here was smack-dab in the middle of this country of ours. I had no idea before that. When they asked me to donate it, I didn't even flinch. I took nothin' for it, either. I believe we need to make exceptions for things like this. There's good that comes out of markers and monuments!

"Take this here spot for instance: folks drivin' through Kansas, they see the sign on the highway, they take a little detour and stop. Spendin' a little extra time, they can say they stood in the exact center of the United States!

"You know," he marveled, "take a look here in this visitors book. People have come here from every state in the union and some foreign countries, too. That's amazin' for a place like this, so far from the big highways. It gives me satisfaction, people takin' the time to come here. It's a tribute.

"Take a good look here in the book: folks from Alabama, New Jersey, here's Hawaii. Now, that's out of the way! If you ask me, this here's a pretty good spot to pull over and rest while you're on your way to somewhere else. And it's something to say you stood right here where I am, smack-dab in the heart of America!"

Cattle Pens, Bazaar, Kansas

Flint Hills, *Cassoday, Kansas*

ALONE ON THE PRAIRIE

Journal Entry: Gove County, 4/26/84

This was my assignment. Go to one uninhabited spot in the wide open spaces and stay there all day—sun-up to dark!

I owed this trip to my belief that life off the beaten path is more genuine. And, besides, loneliness is an aspect of the land. And, for one day, I wanted a full dose of it. Just me and the prairie, that's all!

My equipment: one notepad, one lawn chair, and a clear mind. My destination: Monument Rocks in Gove County, Kansas. Twenty miles from nowhere, these chalkstone monoliths jut right out of the ground as natural wonderments to flatness! They are peculiar remnants for these parts, and the vestige of previous past. They are prehistoric residue and were here millions of years ago when the Great Plains was an enormous inland sea. From afar, these relics appear to have been sculpted by the Creator himself. Up close, they merely bear the stamp of having lasted. Nonetheless, they are significant. They are history. And in them are the ghosts of evolution!

For me in particular, they hold value. Besides being a link to the past, they are a force for me to focus on. So, at the crack of dawn, this balmy, still morning, I pulled off the blacktop north of Scott City and journeyed across the rolling, open plain, spirited, a lone citizen of Mother Earth, intent to learn something about me and my past.

Eight miles later, the dirt road ended. The rest of the way I trekked on foot. Some 100 yards away, I stopped, took in a clean breath, and looked all around. This spot was good . . . as good as any . . . so I stretched, uncranked the chair, and got settled. It was finally time to contemplate the words of the wise men, "knowledge comes from listening" and "to understand silence you must be still." So, with the utmost effort, I began to listen to nothing and tried to be perfectly still. Perched as a lonesome speck between a vacant prairie and an empty sky, I hushed myself and anticipated pure silence.

But there was none!

Even in this remote, seemingly noiseless expanse, I heard things. The humming of flies. The distant bawl of a calf. Grasshoppers with their wild ringing. A lone crow, squawking in the clear sky above me. Even the wind sang as it whistled cleanly through the thistle and clumps of wild brush. The lone prairie was stirring, and this demolished my expectations. All my life, I was sure there was true silence somewhere! But not now. I had to ask myself, "Does it matter?" Solitude itself has virtue. And here, at least, I was alone. And what I was listening for did come through. "Homo sapiens, you are less significant now! In this one place, uninhabited but alive, you are just another kind of creature!"

What an awakening! Out in the middle of this flat scape of sage, wildflowers, and prairie grass, I stood relieved. Actually, redemption is what I felt. With all things equal, I could put to rest my conquering instincts. Now, more than ever, I could feel unbridled, wild, and free! Right here was where I could scrape off my innocence. Right here was where I could unravel myself. And it was time to let myself go.

So, on this prairie, in the middle of nowhere, I made a complete effort to blend in and discover. I stared off far away. I tuned into my heartbeat. I studied my shadow. I felt for the soft pattering of my pulse. I listened to the roar inside my ears. I squinted my eyes, blurring the acute shapes of things around me. I smelled the dirt I had scooped up with my hands. I imagined being the breeze that blew through my shirt. I tried to attach myself to the timeless rhythm of nature—minus man.

I began to act out the free scope given the imagination. I experimented! I closed my eyes, got out of the lawn chair, and walked around. I wanted to be lost. Yet I discovered I could find my way back by the warm direction of the sun. I got up and walked again, further away, until the lawn chair was only a speck on the horizon. As I moved, I listened to the earth crush beneath my feet. I walk heavy. Still, I kept on. I went out far enough that, when I looked back this time, my only possession, the lawn chair, appeared to be at the very edge of the earth.

There was a huge emptiness, and it gave me a surge. For the first time, I was walking where few men had, on the edge of reality. I paused, sucked in the vibrating silence, and felt a power I can still not describe . . . Here was another world, one of free expression. A world where life had no facade and where loneliness itself was the natural price for being alive.

Off in the distance, again I stared intently. I clarified in my vision those huge rocks that hold fossils in them still. They alone were here before anything else. And they alone hold the real secrets of what the prairie and these wide open spaces have forever been about. But, for this instant, I imagined, they would share with me one of their prairie secrets. Out here on the edge, alone and empty, I got this almighty sensation: according to the rocks, right here is where creation began!

Monument Rocks, *Gove County*

Steve Johnson

STEVE JOHNSON

Journal Entry: Mitchell, Nebraska, 6/7/83

Steve Johnson is a rancher, the kind you don't see any more: independent, with no strings attached. What he does is real cowboy stuff. I was with him at his round-up, and I watched him move with a hard layer of confidence. He's a shaker. He makes things happen.

There's a butte on Steve Johnson's ranch that overlooks some of the most wide-open, well-defined country I've ever seen. Steve goes up to the butte for inspiration. At the end of this day, long because of branding cattle, Steve took me along.

"You've got to have a place like this," said Steve. "To me a man needs two things: a place he can go and someone he can look up to. I'm lucky, I've got both.

"My dad is who I look up to. Chief is the man I admire. He has guided me along the right way. He was never overbearing. He let me think for myself. He's just watched over me and kept me steered straight. He let it be up to me to come back to ranching. I'll never forget that. When I come up here, I always think about how I was raised."

"Amazing," I replied. "I was guided the right way, too. My dad was a rare person. He cared about people. His friends were his prized possessions. To this day, he holds a special memory and an honored spot in many hearts. Because of him, I learned to value people and be my own man. Now that I'm grown, I realize he was the great teacher in my life."

Steve and I sat quiet for a while, and as the sun faded toward Wyoming and with my adrenalin still pumping on heartfelt words, something hit me hard.

Here I was, in a frontier country with someone I hardly knew, and we were having an honest-to-goodness, heart-to-heart talk. It was hard to believe. Men don't do this. Men don't show their emotions. But up here, in this setting, the tough crust of the male ego crumbled away. Steve and I shared secrets. Under some pretty tough skin, emotions poured out. Two grown men coming of age.

This was new territory for me, but I'll never forget it. Not this day, this butte, and this rancher. Together, they brought me a moment I will always go back to. A moment when a deeper part of my life came full circle.

It's a spot, too, I will save for my dad. Walt would have relished a scene like this. It's because of him I even met a man like Steve Johnson.

THE COLLECTOR AND HIS B-52

Journal Entry: Harlan, Kansas, 9/26/82

*T*he old Nichols Country Store had things in it, on it, and around it in great quantities. "I've been here fifty-three years," said Kelly Nichols, "collectin' ever'day."

Right here is apparently the drop-off point for things "unwanted." I never saw a place so jam-packed with relics. Kelly Nichols will take in anything with slightly higher status than junk. "It comes in and goes out ever'day."

Among the assemblage of "saved things" he showed me were books, bottles, boxes, buckets, batteries, coolers, crates, plates, signs, implements, boxes of you-name-it, plus a few antiques . . . and, up in the rafters, surrounded by cobwebs and all by itself, was this stuffed goose.

"Where did you get that thing?"

"That Canadian, my B-52! I shot him out of the sky in 1977. You ever shot a goose? It ain't easy. Seldom do ya get the chance. If you ain't a hunter, I gotta tell ya, bringing down a Canadian is the ultimate!

"I was up to Glen Elder Reservoir in some shallows amongst the reeds. I had my 10-gauge double barrel with me, and this 'un flew right over me. He was so big he looked like a bomber. These things make ducks look like sparrows. That's why we call 'em B-52s. They're huge . . . Anyway, he came in to land, and I nailed him. It was a thrill, I tell ya. I stuffed him and hung him up here in the rafters all by himself. This here's the only time he's ever been moved, his only flight since D-Day."

"You wouldn't part with him either, I'll bet?"

"Nope, you're right there. Wouldn't dare! Whatever I collect is for sale. But not my goose. This here's a trophy. My B-52, it's the only one I'll ever collect!"

Kelly Nichols, The Collector

WALLY LATTIMER
AND A LITTLE HOMEGROWN PHILOSOPHY

Journal Entry: Lyons, Kansas, 10/29/82

I was born in 1881 in Illinois. I came to Kansas when I was five. I've lived here in Lyons since 1916, and I first remember votin' in 19 and 4. I put an "X" for Teddy Roosevelt. People like me to tell 'em my facts. I'm the oldest living person they know. Matter of fact, I'm the oldest living person I know."

Wally Lattimer knows his own reputation. He's a legend in the Midwest. He's been on "Hee-Haw" three times and Johnny Carson twice. He's spoken with the secretary of agriculture and he knows the governor. In Lyons, they have Wally Lattimer Day every year. "And they'll keep on havin' it 'til they bury me," laughed Wally.

"Since I've been to Hollywood," he boasted, "I put Lyons on the map. They like me on them shows 'cause I'm outspoken. I don't get stage fright. I speak my mind. I don't act humble because I'm in Hollywood. I'll tell ya something. Johnny Carson and Grandpa Jones, they put their pants on just like you and me. Money and television don't make 'em better people. We're all the same in my book."

Wally stays active. He showed me where he farms 105 acres of wheat, where he tends a seven-acre garden of vegetables, and two acres of nothing but petunias. He said he figures he wears out a garden hoe every seventeen to twenty years. Having survived two wives, his best companions now are his nine children, nineteen grandchildren, and thirty-nine great-grandchildren.

"I've been a bachelor for twelve years, and I'm still going strong. I still don't need glasses, and I love to read. Non-fiction is my thing. *National Geographic*. I love facts. I've educated myself reading. The only thing better is travel. I love sights. I've seen the world. I've done 48,000 miles in cruises."

"You've sure been around, Wally. Now, you know, I'm wondering how you do it. What keeps you going so strong?"

"Well, here's a little of my homegrown philosophy. I'll tell ya like I tell ever'body.

"People look at me and wonder how I do it. My main lesson in life is simple. Take it one day at a time. But along with that, I got a few rules I follow. I eat right. I don't smoke. I might drink a beer, but not another one! I never tell a lie because I believe in the truth. And I believe in people."

"You got it right, Wally. That ought to be etched in stone: 'Wally's Homegrown Philosophy.' "

It must work. At this writing, Wally Lattimer is 101 and going strong.

Wally Lattimer

Clifford Stipps

MY PHILOSOPHY
by CLIFFORD STIPPS

Journal Entry: Ottawa, 11/13/82

I'm gettin' on," said Clifford Stipps, "but I ain't about to act it. That's the wrong way to live. My philosophy is this: You feel how you want to feel. Age don't mean you're old. You can be as young as you want.

"You know how I stay young? I keep up with the kids. I work out with the wrestlers down at the school. I get a kick out of 'em. They got spunk. They make me feel young. Old people ought to go back to school, not to study, but to hang around and get a rubbin' from the kids.

"I've got another rule about gettin' on. I stay clear away from the moaners and the groaners. I don't like to listen to aches and pains. People who talk about problems just get more. If you talk doom of gloom, then you end up livin' it.

"My philosophy is to stay away from the groaners and start out the day right. I've got a book I keep on my kitchen table right by the toaster. I've never read it, but that's not why it's there. It's the title that gets me goin'. It's my motto. I read it every day. First thing every morning, I get goin' at the kitchen table by readin' the title of that book, *He Can Who Thinks He Can.* Ain't that a way to start a day!"

Lowell Thierer

LOWELL THIERER

Journal Entry: Alma, Kansas, Molasses Day 1980

I went to the Lowell Thierer farm for the seventeenth annual celebration of Molasses Day. Lowell calls it his fall extravaganza. Molasses made the old way. Even before the gates were opened, Lowell was humming. The first thing he did was take me down to his sorghum patch.

"This here is how molasses begins," he explained. "Sorghum is the raw material. Get a picture of me in front of my patch, would ya? It sure grew tall this year."

After showing me the sorghum patch, Lowell took me up to the shed where he refines his molasses and puts it in jars to sell.

"These jars will all be gone by tomorrow," bragged Lowell. "We go back in time. On our molasses we use copper, a wood fire, and a lot of stirrin'.

"Molasses Day keeps gettin' bigger," he went on, " 'cause it reminds folks of the good ol' days. My wife Myrtle, she spins yarn for folks up at the shop on the hill. Bud, my boy, runs an old print press, and I haul people around in a wagon behind my '23 Rumely Oil Pull. This day was designed to bring back memories. We make a little money, but mostly it's for goin' back and havin' fun."

Lowell made me stick with him all day. I drove the Rumely, ran the press, and stirred the molasses. He couldn't figure someone from my generation being so interested in going back in time. I said to him, "You can't know where you're going unless you know where you've been."

"That's right," he beamed. "You got to know your roots!"

After a whole day of nostalgia and a free jar of molasses, I was content. I couldn't ask for more. I was about to leave when a neighbor cornered me and asked, "What did you think?"

"Molasses Day was great," I told him. "I drove the Rumely, ran the press, and learned everything there is to know about molasses."

"No, about Lowell," he said. "What did you think of Lowell?"

"Oh, Lowell," I grinned. "Let me tell you, after today, I feel like family. He treated me like a son."

He laughed. "Lowell's that way. One time he drove 20 miles out of his way to help me fix a flat, on the condition I go back to his place and have supper. I did, and we stayed up all night tellin' stories and goin' back in time."

Open Road

TOBE ZWEYGARDT

Journal Entry: St. Francis, Kansas, 7/29/83

I've got a huge amount of respect for someone who can pick up a piece of scrap iron and make something out of it. Tobe Zweygardt can do that.

He caught my eye at a folk life festival. He had a booth full of sculptures made of barnyard debris: barbwire, horseshoes, railroad spikes, and the like. The things he made stood out. You could see his heart was in them. Anyone could see that. That's art to me, when you put your heart into something. Tobe's an artist. He can take a piece of junk and give it life.

There was something about him I wanted to discover, so I went to St. Francis, Kansas. That's where I found that his vitality is contagious. Tobe Zweygardt has not lost the fire of life. He still craves adventure. He still goes exploring. Today, Tobe took me to Horse Thief Canyon and Beecher's Island; then he took me arrowhead hunting.

"You find arrowheads in high places," he said. "Abandoned lookouts, that's where. You imagine being an Indian up there, looking out and looking around in all directions."

We went up to a high plain north of town. There, we scoured around for arrowheads.

Tobe said, "This is a perfect spot. Look around now for burnt stone and broken rock. Look where the ground's a little dark. An Indian has been where the ground's dark. Look here, this is a spot. A scout was here, had a fire, and made arrowheads. This is where we'll kick around. Maybe something will turn up. You can find 'em. I have. Think like an Indian."

Tobe amazed me with his knowledge. He shared with me his every secret about arrowheads, the hills around St. Francis, and the history of these parts. "They're worth the passing on," he told me. "You gotta stay close to your history."

The time went quickly. Tobe's energy engulfed me. He got excited everytime he spoke about the hills and their history. He reminded me of my mentor Walt. The distinct face. The penetrating eyes. The belief that true friends shared things and gave freely. With either of them a walk, a drive, a conversation, anything could mean excitement.

Tobe saved his best place for last. It was near the homestead where he was brought up. It is where the sweep of history comes to him. The spot is a rocky bluff that overlooks a ravine of wild plums and a field of tall prairie grass. It's where historians claim the last buffalo was "run to death" in Kansas. And it's where Tobe's family came and went. He recounted the details for me. The stories and this spot absorbed him.

"The older I've gotten," he recalled, "and the more I've seen change, the more I've come to appreciate special places. This here's one. This is my spot, my sacred place."

We just stood there a while, feeling Tobe's spot and gazing at that land. I photographed him there. Then I scribbled in my journal, "People who keep their history acquire a look that's rarely found."

Coming down off that bluff, Tobe put an arrowhead in my hand. "You keep this. Keep it as a reminder of all the history that's out here in these hills. One thing, though, just promise me you'll pass it on. The arrowhead and the history."

Tobe Zweygardt

The Prairie

GEMS

Journal Entry: The Prairie, 10/16/86

*J*oe Walker spoke of gems. The kind you find in your own backyard, the kind that live and breathe: homo sapiens.

Joe said, "The best people in the whole world are your own neighbors. They're like diamonds in the rough. Gems . . . what you gotta do is uncover 'em, meet 'em, get to know 'em—you'll be better for it!"

Joe's right. There are gems out there, and they are as bright and shining as the windswept plain. I have found them everywhere—illuminating. Uncovering them has gotten into my blood. For me, gem hunting has become an affair of the heart. From it I have gained new respect for the value of people and the spirit of place. Adventuring for gems has given true meaning to the virtue of "roaming, hoping never to arrive," because I have found gems where you would least expect them: in between destinations and off the beaten path, in the quieter parts of America. They are out there just waiting to be discovered. As one man I met, who closed his shop and went looking for America, put it, "What really stirred me was the people I met—people with dreams!"

Chasing after gems, I have gotten a close look at people with dreams, and I have found a true quality in them. They are realists. They have a certain restless energy, an energy pioneers used to call "looking for elephants," which to them meant pushing on, going over the next hill, chasing after the next horizon, for that is where dreams are made. The gems I have found know full well that today's dreams lay waiting on tomorrow's horizons. To live your dream, you make your life in the chase, always after the next horizon, forever pushing on. For it is in the chase where energy becomes restless and new dreams are born. In the process of "looking for elephants" and chasing after dreams, a certain courage is built, the courage that forms the character of an open kind of country.

Out of the process of uncovering gems, I've learned lessons from the prairie and its people, lessons etched in my mind, lessons to keep in my heart. For it was proven to me that dreams *can* be made. I have been taught you can know little of someone and still gain their trust. The people of the prairie have reacquainted me with discovery. About them I have learned something of what it takes to last. They have shown me that ordinary life is significant.

In frozen moments I can look back and pick out my ordinary heroes. I can see them before my very eyes. They are the real people I've met, folks who have kept what they've grown up with. On the plains they are the souls who still honor a handshake, the ones who still help their neighbor, people who still give their word and stand by it. To them everyday life is still old-fashioned, and they are proud of it. Their language has a pure kind of ring to it. They work at getting to the bottom of things. They have emotions that bare quickly. And their territory is a place where everything can come straight from the heart. They and their country are one.

I have felt its pulse, and this flat kind of country has its own brand of magic. A romanticism spelled out in effort. A spirit that must be explored. For when you truly explore the prairie, it can force awakening. If you dig deep enough and peel enough away, you can reach a level of truth that is authentic and the pure essence of our past.

Today, as we bolt ahead full tilt toward tomorrow, we are leaving in our wake something vital: our heritage. The roads we never go down, the little towns we never visit, and the gems we never meet: they are America. And they are the proof that America is still beautiful and the human spirit has no size.

"It was a dream that brought us here,"
said a pioneer, "and it's a dream we gotta pass on!"

LYLE ALAN WHITE

Future Gems

LIST OF PHOTOGRAPHS